Webster's

21ST CENTURY

Book of Quotations

Webster's

21ST CENTURY
Book of Quotations

THOMAS NELSON PUBLISHERS
Nashville

Published in Nashville, Tennessee, by Thomas Nelson, Inc., Publishers and distributed in Canada by Lawson Falle, Ltd., Cambridge, Ontario.

Printed in the United States of America.

Library of Congress Cataloging-in-Publication Data

Webster's 21st century book of quotations.
p. cm.—(21st century desk reference set)
ISBN 0-8407-4256-8 (HB—Burgundy)
0-8407-4233-9 (HB—Navy)
0-8407-3478-6 (PB)
1. Quotations, English. I. Thomas Nelson Publishers. II. Title: Webster's twenty-first century book of quotations. III. Series.
PN6081.W36 1992
808.88′2—dc20
91–46650
CIP

1 2 3 4 5 6 7 8 9 10 — 99 98 97 96 95 94 93 92

A

Ability

See also: Character; Genius; Perseverance; Power; Strength; Success

Natural abilities are like natural plants; they need pruning by study.

—Francis Bacon

Ability is commonly found to consist mainly in a big degree of solemnity.

—Ambrose Bierce

The question "Who ought to be boss?" is like asking "Who ought to be the tenor in the quartet?" Obviously, the man who can sing tenor.

—Henry Ford

There is something that is much more scarce, something finer far, something rarer than ability. It is the ability to recognize ability.

—Elbert Hubbard

Talent without genius isn't much, but genius without talent is nothing whatever.

—Paul Valéry

Intelligence is quickness to apprehend, as distinct from ability, which is capacity to act wisely on the thing apprehended.

—A. N. Whitehead

Absence

See also: Loneliness

I was court-martialled in my absence, and sentenced to death in my absence, so I said they could shoot me in my absence.

—Brendan Behan

Absence blots people out. We really have no absent friends.

—Elizabeth Bowen

Absence diminishes minor passions and inflames great ones, as the wind douses a candle and fans a fire.

—François, Duc de La Rochefoucauld

Is not absence death to those who love?

—Alexander Pope

Judicious absence is a weapon.

—Charles Reade

Abuse

The greater the power, the more dangerous the abuse.

—Edmund Burke

It seldom pays to be rude. It never pays to be only half-rude.

—Norman Douglas

Humor is a drug which it's the fashion to abuse.

—Sir William Schwenck Gilbert

Abuse is the weapon of the vulgar.

—Samuel Griswold Goodrich

A fly, Sir, may sting a stately horse and make him wince; but one is but an insect, and the other is a horse still.

—Samuel Johnson

The highest proof of virtue is to possess boundless power without abusing it.

—Lord Macaulay

Abuse resembles a church procession; it always returns to the point from which it set out.

—Monti

Accomplishment/Achievement

See also: Fame; Success; Work

The test of a vocation is the love of the drudgery it involves.

—Anonymous

If you think you can, you can. And if you think you can't, you're right.

—Mary Kay Ash

It is all very well to be able to write books, but can you waggle your ears?

—J. M. Barrie

One never notices what has been done; one can only see what remains to be done.

—Marie Curie

The reward of a thing well done, is to have done it.

—Ralph Waldo Emerson

If you cannot work with love but only with distaste, it is better that you should leave your work and sit at the gates of the temple and take alms of those who work with joy.

—Kahlil Gibran

My mother drew a distinction between achievement and success. She said that achievement is the knowledge that you have studied and worked hard and done the best that is in you. Success is being praised by others, and that's nice, too, but not as important or satisfying. Always aim for achievement and forget about success.

—Helen Hayes

Every calling is great when greatly pursued.

—Oliver Wendell Holmes

Those that have done nothing in life are not qualified to judge of those that have done little.

—Samuel Johnson

One can never consent to creep when one feels an impulse to soar.

—Helen Keller

I feel that the greatest reward for doing is the opportunity to do more.

—Jonas Salk

I do want to get rich, but I never want to do what there is to do to get rich.

—*Gertrude Stein*

The youth gets together his materials to build a bridge to the moon, or, perchance, a palace or temple on the earth, and, at length, the middle-aged man concludes to build a woodshed with them.

—*Henry David Thoreau*

To achieve great things we must live as though we were never going to die.

—*Marquis de Vauvenargues*

Actors and Acting

See: Arts: Drama and Acting

Adversity

See: Trouble

Advertising

Advertising is 85% confusion and 15% commission.

—*Fred Allen*

Any publicity is good publicity.

—*Anonymous*

Sanely applied advertising could remake the world.

—*Stuart Chase*

You can tell the ideals of a nation by its advertisements.

—Norman Douglas

Advertisements contain the only truth to be relied on in the newspaper.

—Thomas Jefferson

Advertising may be described as the science of arresting the human intelligence long enough to get money from it.

—Stephen Butler Leacock

Advertising is a valuable economic factor because it is the cheapest way of selling goods, particularly if the goods are worthless.

—Sinclair Lewis

Ads are the cave art of the twentieth century.

—Marshall McLuhan

Advertising is the rattling of a stick inside a swill bucket.

—George Orwell

Let advertisers spend the same amount of money improving their product as they do on advertising, and they wouldn't have to advertise it.

—Will Rogers

Advertising is the art of making whole lies out of half truths.

—Edgar Shoaff

Advice

Good advice is one of those insults that ought to be forgiven.

—Anonymous

Advice is like castor oil, easy enough to give but dreadful uneasy to take.

—Josh Billings

Never go to a doctor whose office plants are dead.

—Erma Bombeck

In those days he was wiser than he is now—he used frequently to take my advice.

—Winston Churchill

Advice is like snow; the softer it falls the longer it dwells upon, and the deeper it sinks into the mind.

—Samuel Taylor Coleridge

Old people like to give good advice, as solace for no longer being able to provide bad example.

—François, Duc de La Rochefoucauld

A good scare is worth more to a man than good advice.

—E. W. Howe

No one wants advice—only corroboration.

—John Steinbeck

The only thing to do with good advice is to pass it on. It is never of any use to oneself.

—Oscar Wilde

Age and Aging

See also: Maturity

To me, old age is always fifteen years older than I am.

—Bernard Baruch

We grow neither better nor worse as we get old, but more like ourselves.

—May Lamberton Becker

Old age is not so bad when you consider the alternative.

—Maurice Chevalier

Age does not depend upon years, but upon temperament and health. Some men are born old, and some never grow so.

—Tryon Edwards

Setting a good example for your children takes all the fun out of middle age.

—William Feather

One of the many things nobody ever tells you about middle age is that it's such a nice change from being young.

—Dorothy Canfield Fisher

Forty is the old age of youth; fifty is the youth of old age.

—Victor Hugo

Youth had been a habit of hers for so long that she could not part with it.

—Rudyard Kipling

There is a fountain of youth: it is your mind, your talents, the creativity you bring to your life and the lives of people you love. When you learn to tap this source, you will have truly defeated age.

—Sophia Loren

Middle age is the time when a man is always thinking that in a week or two he will feel as good as ever.

—Don Marquis

I wish it were OK in this country to look one's age, whatever it is. Maturity has a lot going for it, even in terms of esthetics. For example, you no longer get bubblegum stuck in your braces.

—Cyra McFadden

After a certain number of years, our faces become our biographies.

—Cynthia Ozick

From birth to age 18, a girl needs good parents, from 18 to 35 she needs good looks, from 35 to 55 she needs a good personality, and from 55 on she needs cash.

—Sophie Tucker

I am not young enough to know everything.

—*Oscar Wilde*

Agreement

When you say that you agree to a thing in principle you mean that you have not the slightest intention of carrying it out in practice.

—*Otto von Bismarck*

My idea of an agreeable person is a person who agrees with me.

—*Benjamin Disraeli*

What were politicians? A politician was a person with whose politics you did not agree. When you did agree, he was a statesman.

—*David Lloyd George*

Men are much more apt to agree in what they do than in what they think.

—*Johann Wolfgang von Goethe*

There is nothing more likely to drive a man mad than . . . an obstinate, constitutional preference of the true to the agreeable.

—*William Hazlitt*

It is my melancholy fate to like so many people I profoundly disagree with and often heartily dislike people who agree with me.

—*Mary Kingsley*

Agree with thine adversary quickly, whiles thou art in the way with him.

—*Matthew 13:25*

We seldom attribute common sense except to those who agree with us.

—*François, Duc de la Rochefoucauld*

Few are qualified to shine in company; but it is most men's power to be agreeable.

—*Jonathan Swift*

Ah! don't say you agree with me. When people agree with me I always feel that I must be wrong.

—*Oscar Wilde*

If two men on the same job agree all the time, then one is useless. If they disagree all the time, then both are useless.

—*Darryl F. Zanuck*

Ambition

See also: Boldness and Initiative; Vanity

Ambition. An overmastering desire to be vilified by enemies while living and made ridiculous by friends when dead.

—*Ambrose Bierce*

No bird soars too high if he soars with his own wings.

—*William Blake*

The slave has but one master; the ambitious man has as many as can help in making his fortune.

—Jean de la Bruyère

All ambitions are lawful except those which climb upward on the miseries or credulities of mankind.

—Joseph Conrad

It is never too late to be what you might have been.

—George Eliot

Hitch your wagon to a star.

—Ralph Waldo Emerson

By working faithfully eight hours per day, you may eventually get to be a boss and work twelve hours a day.

—Robert Frost

Ambition has one heel nailed in well, though she stretches her fingers to touch the heavens.

—William Lilly

Most people would succeed in small things if they were not troubled with great ambitions.

—Henry Wadsworth Longfellow

Ours is a world where people don't know what they want and are willing to go through hell to get it.

—Don Marquis

Everybody sets out to do something, and everybody does something, but no one does what he sets out to do.

—George Moore

The very substance of the ambitious is merely the shadow of a dream.

—William Shakespeare

Ambition often puts men upon doing the meanest offices: so climbing is performed in the same posture with creeping.

—Jonathan Swift

Keep away from people who try to belittle your ambitions. Small people always do that, but the really great make you feel that you, too, can become great.

—Mark Twain

You can't hold a man down without staying down with him.

—Booker T. Washington

Ambition is the last refuge of failure.

—Oscar Wilde

America and Americans

America is the only nation in history which, miraculously, has gone directly from barbarism to degeneration without the usual interval of civilization.

—George Clemenceau

Americans are like a rich father who wishes he knew how to give his sons the hardships that made him rich.

—Robert Frost

Our country is the world—our countrymen are all mankind.

—William Lloyd Garrison

Ours is the only country deliberately founded on a good idea.

—John Gunther

For other nations, utopia is a blessed past never to be recovered; for Americans it is just beyond the horizon.

—Henry Kissinger

Intellectually, I know that America is no better than any other country. Emotionally, I know she is better than every other country.

—Sinclair Lewis

American women expect to find in their husbands a perfection that English women only hope to find in their butlers.

—W. Somerset Maugham

Since the earliest days of our frontier irreverence has been one of the signs of our affection.

—Dean Rusk

America is a large, friendly dog in a very small room. Every time it wags its tail it knocks over a chair.

—Arnold Joseph Toynbee

Of course, America had often been discovered before, but it had always been hushed up.

—Oscar Wilde

Ancestry

People will not look forward to posterity, who never looked backward to their ancestors.

—Edmund Burke

There is no king who has not had a slave amongst his ancestors, and no slave who has not had a king among his.

—Helen Keller

I don't know who my grandfather was; I am much more concerned to know what his grandson will be.

—Abraham Lincoln

The sharp thorn often produces delicate roses.

—Ovid

It is indeed a desirable thing to be well-descended, but the glory belongs to our ancestors.

—Plutarch

My folks didn't come over on the *Mayflower,* but they were there to meet the boat.

—Will Rogers

If you cannot get rid of the family skeleton, you may as well make it dance.

—George Bernard Shaw

Anger

See also: Hate; Violence

The angry people are those people who are most afraid.

—Dr. Robert Anthony

Never go to bed mad. Stay up and fight.

—Phyllis Diller

Beware the fury of a patient man.

—John Dryden

To rule one's anger is well; to prevent it is still better.

—Tyron Edwards

Anger is one of the sinews of the soul; he that lacks it has a maimed mind.

—Thomas Fuller

Anger is a momentary madness, so control your passion or it will control you.

—Horace

The flame of anger, bright and brief, sharpens the barb of love.

—Walter S. Landor

No man can think clearly when his fists are clenched.

—George Jean Nathan

Think when you are enraged at anyone, what would probably become of your sentiments should he die during the dispute.

—William Shenstone

Annunciation

See: Jesus Christ

Appearances

See also: Dress; Style

The bosom can ache beneath diamond brooches; and many a blithe heart dances under coarse wool.

—Edwin Hubbel Chapin

Appearances are not held to be a clue to the truth. But we seem to have no other.

—Ivy Compton-Burnett

Getting talked about is one of the penalties for being pretty, while being above suspicion is about the only compensation for being homely.

—Kin Hubbard

Ugliness is a point of view: an ulcer is wonderful to a pathologist.

—Austin O'Malley

You may turn into an archangel, a fool, or a criminal—no one will see it. But when a button is missing—everyone sees that.

—Erich M. Remarque

Things are entirely what they appear to be and behind them . . . there is nothing.

—Jean Paul Sartre

The world is governed more by appearances than by realities, so that it is fully as necessary to seem to know something as to know it.

—Daniel Webster

It is only shallow people who do not judge by appearances.

—Oscar Wilde

Appeasement

See also: Obedience; Peace

Appeasers believe that if you keep on throwing steaks to a tiger, the tiger will turn vegetarian.

—Heywood Broun

An appeaser is one who feeds a crocodile, hoping it will eat him last.

—Winston Churchill

Architecture
See: Arts: Architecture

Armies
See: War

Arts

With an apple I will astonish Paris.

—Paul Cezanne

Art, like morality, consists of drawing the line somewhere.

—G. K. Chesterton

I do not paint a portrait to look like the subject, rather does the person grow to look like his portrait.

—Salvador Dali

In the art world, creativity involves aesthetic sensibility, emotional resonance and a gift for expression.

—Edward DeBono

Art is a jealous mistress, and if a man has a genius for painting, poetry, music, architecture or philosophy, he makes a bad husband and an ill provider.

—Ralph Waldo Emerson

In his work, the artist should be like God in creation: invisible and all-powerful. He should be felt everywhere and seen nowhere.

—Gustave Flaubert

If art is to nourish the roots of our culture, society must set the artist free to follow his vision wherever it takes him.

—*John F. Kennedy*

Art is the expression of an enormous preference.

—*Wyndham Lewis*

All art is a revolt against man's fate.

—*André Malraux*

Art is not an end in itself, but a means of addressing humanity.

—*Modest Mussorgsky*

We have art, in order not to die of the truth.

—*Nietzsche*

Art washes away from the soul the dust of everyday life.

—*Picasso*

Art is lies that tell the truth.

—*Picasso*

If my husband would ever meet a woman on the street who looked like the women in his paintings, he would fall over in a dead faint.

—*Mrs. Pablo Picasso*

Art disease is caused by a hardening of the categories.

—*Adina Reinhardt*

Art is a delayed echo.

—*George Santayana*

Painting is silent poetry; poetry is painting that speaks.

—Simonides

Art is an attitude toward life. If you aim your work and your life high, keep your scene harmonious, then you're an artist and your life is art.

—Gage Taylor

Arts: Architecture

Architecture is inhabited sculpture.

—Constantin Brancusi

A large number of us have developed a feeling that architects tend to design houses for the approval of fellow architects and critics—not for the tenants.

—Charles, Prince of Wales

Architecture is the art of how to waste space

—Philip Johnson

No person who is not a great sculptor or painter can be an architect. If he is not a sculptor or painter, he can only be a builder.

—John Ruskin

Architecture in general is frozen music.

—Friedrich Wilhelm Joseph von Schelling

Arts: Drama and Acting

An actor's success has the life expectancy of a small boy about to look into a gas tank with a lighted match.

—Fred Allen

Acting is the ability to keep an audience from coughing.

—Jean-Louis Barrault

I never said that all actors are cattle; what I said was that all actors should be treated like cattle.

—Alfred Hitchcock

We wear the robes that we have designed for ourselves, and then act out other people's fantasies.

—Laurence Olivier

The stage is actor's country. You have to get your passport stamped every so often or they take away your citizenship.

—Vanessa Redgrave

As long as more people will pay admission to a theater to see a naked body than to see a naked brain, the drama will languish.

—George Bernard Shaw

Drama is what you do when you have a dream while you're awake.

—Ron Smothermon

Acting is not an important job in the scheme of things. Plumbing is.

—Spencer Tracy

The world is a comedy to those who think and a tragedy to those who feel.

—Horace Walpole

Arts: Music and Dance

I just put my feet in the air and move them around.

—Fred Astaire

I wish Frank Sinatra would just shut up and sing.

—Lauren Bacall

I don't want people who want to dance, I want people who have to dance.

—George Balanchine

Music has charms to soothe a savage breast.

—William Congreve

The body never lies.

—Martha Graham

Ballet is the ectoplasm of music.

—Russell Green

Classical music is the kind that we keep hoping will turn into a tune.

—Kin Hubbard

After silence that which comes nearest to expressing the inexpressible is music.

—Aldous Huxley

Music is the only language in which you cannot say a mean or sarcastic thing.

—Lord Erskine

Wagner's music is better than it sounds.

—Mark Twain

An unalterable and unquestioned law of the musical world required that the German text of French operas sung by Swedish artists should be translated into Italian for the clear understanding of English speaking audiences.

—Edith Wharton

Arts: Poetry and Poets

Being a professor of poetry is rather like being a Kentucky colonel. It's not really a subject one can profess—unless one hires oneself out to write pieces for funerals or the marriages of dons.

—W. H. Auden

Poetry is the art of substantiating shadows, and of lending existence to nothing.

—Edmund Burke

Free verse is like free love; it is a contradiction in terms.

—G. K. Chesterton

Idleness, that is the curse of other men, is the nurse of poets.

—Walter D'Arcy Cresswell

If . . . it makes my whole body so cold no fire can warm me, I know that is poetry.

—Emily Dickinson

Immature poets imitate; mature poets steal.

—T. S. Eliot

Writing free verse is like playing tennis with the net down.

—Robert Frost

To be a poet is a condition rather than a profession.

—Robert Graves

There's no money in poetry, but there's no poetry in money either.

—Robert Graves

You will not find poetry anywhere unless you bring some of it with you.

—Joseph Joubert

When power leads man toward arrogance, poetry reminds him of his limitations. When power narrows the areas of man's concern, poetry reminds him of the richness and diversity of his existence. When power corrupts, poetry cleanses.

—John F. Kennedy

Publishing a volume of verse is like dropping a rose petal down the Grand Canyon and waiting for the echo.

—Don Marquis

Poetry is a mixture of common sense, which not all have, with an uncommon sense, which very few have.

—John Masefield

Poets utter great and wise things which they do not themselves understand.

—Plato

With me poetry has not been a purpose, but a passion.

—Edgar Allan Poe

One merit of poetry few persons will deny: it says more and in fewer words than prose.

—Voltaire

All bad poetry springs from genuine feeling.

—Oscar Wilde

Arts: Writing

See also: Books and Reading; Language; Literature

If you can't annoy somebody, there's little point in writing.

—Kingsley Amis

No iron can pierce the heart with such force as a period put just at the right place.

—Isaac Babel

I do most of my work sitting down; that's where I shine.

—Robert Benchley

Better to write for yourself and have no public, than to write for the public and have no self.

—Cyril Connolly

Every novel should have a beginning, a muddle, and an end.

—Peter De Vries

Writing is easy: all you do is sit staring at the blank sheet of paper until the drops of blood form on your forehead.

—Gene Fowler

The only sensible ends of literature are, first, the pleasurable toil of writing; second, the gratification of one's family and friends; and, lastly, the solid cash.

—Nathaniel Hawthorne

All books are either dreams or swords,
You can cut or you can drug with words.

—Amy Lowell

The great thing about writing: stay with it . . . ultimately you teach yourself something very important about yourself.

—Bernard Malamud

The only time I know that something is true is the moment I discover it in the act of writing.

—Jean Malaquais

If you want to get rich from writing, write the sort of thing that's read by persons who move their lips when they're reading to themselves.

—Don Marquis

There are three rules for writing a novel. Unfortunately, no one knows what they are.

—W. Somerset Maugham

To write simply is as difficult as to be good.

—W. Somerset Maugham

Writing is the only thing that, when I do it, I don't feel I should be doing something else.

—Gloria Steinem

The difference between the right word and the almost right word is the difference between lightning and the lightning bug.

—Mark Twain

Writing is so difficult that I feel that writers, having had their hell on earth, will escape all punishment hereafter.

—Jessamyn West

Atheism

See also: Skepticism

A little philosophy inclineth man's mind to atheism, but depth in philosophy bringeth men's minds about to religion.

—Francis Bacon

Nobody talks so constantly about God as those who insist that there is no God.

—Heywood Broun

An atheist is a man who has no invisible means of support.

—John Buchan

I don't believe in God because I don't believe in Mother Goose.

—Clarence Darrow

There are so few atheists in the world because it takes more credulity to accept the atheistic position than most men can muster.

—Gerald Kennedy

There are no atheists in the foxholes of Bataan.

—Douglas MacArthur

Absolute atheism starts in an act of faith in reverse gear and is a full-blown religious commitment.

—Jacques Maritain

B

Babies

See: Children and Childhood

Bachelors

It is a truth universally acknowledged that a single man in possession of a good fortune must be in want of a wife.

—Jane Austen

Bachelors know more about women than married men; if they didn't, they'd be married, too.

—H. L. Mencken

Being a bachelor is the first requisite of the man who wishes to form an ideal home.

—Beverly Nichols

A bachelor never quite gets over the idea that he is a thing of beauty and a boy for ever.

—Helen Rowland

Call no man unhappy until he's married.

—Socrates

By persistently remaining single a man converts himself into a permanent public temptation.

—Oscar Wilde

Rich bachelors should be heavily taxed. It is not fair that some men should be happier than others.

—Oscar Wilde

Beauty

See also: Grace; Women

People see you as an object, not as a person, and they project a set of expectations onto you. People who don't have it think beauty is a blessing, but actually it sets you apart.

—Candice Bergen

Beauty is not caused. It is.

—Emily Dickinson

Plain women know more about men than beautiful ones do.

—Katharine Hepburn

Nothing's beautiful from every point of view.

—Horace

Beauty is only skin deep, but it's a valuable asset if you're poor or haven't any sense.

—Kin Hubbard

I'm tired of all this nonsense about beauty being only skin-deep. That's deep enough. What do you want, an adorable pancreas?

—Jean Kerr

All God's children are not beautiful. Most of God's children are, in fact, barely presentable.

—Fran Lebowitz

People who are very beautiful make their own laws.

—Vivien Leigh

One cannot collect all the beautiful shells on the beach. One can collect only a few, and they are more beautiful if they are few.

—Anne Morrow Lindbergh

Beauty is how you feel inside, and it reflects in your eyes. It is not something physical.

—Sophia Loren

Beauty is the purgation of superfluities.

—Michelangelo

No one ever called me pretty when I was a little girl.

—Marilyn Monroe

There are no ugly women, only lazy ones.

—Helena Rubinstein

Beauty is that which excites the soul.

—Gage Taylor

If truth is beauty, how come no one has their hair done in a library?

—Lily Tomlin

Bed

The happiest part of a man's life is what he passes lying awake in bed in the morning.

—Samuel Johnson

I have, all my life long, been lying till noon; yet I tell all young men, and tell them with great sincerity, that nobody who does not rise early will ever do any good.

—Samuel Johnson

Believe me, you have to get up early if you want to get out of bed.

—Groucho Marx

It was such a lovely day I thought it was a pity to get up.

—W. Somerset Maugham

Early to bed and early to rise, makes a man healthy, wealthy, and wise.

—Proverb

Early to rise and early to bed makes a male healthy and wealthy and dead.

—James Thurber

Behavior

See also: Manners

He who takes a stand is often wrong, but he who fails to take a stand is always wrong.

—Anonymous

Live so that you can at least get the benefit of the doubt.

—Kin Hubbard

Be nice to people on your way up because you'll meet them on your way down.

—Wilson Mizner

There are some people who are very resourceful at being resourceful and who apparently feel that the best way to make friends is to do something terrible and then to make amends.

—Ogden Nash

With a gentleman I am always a gentleman and a half, and with a fraud I try to be a fraud and a half.

—Otto von Bismarck

I don't say we all ought to misbehave, but we ought to look as if we could.

—Orson Welles

Belief

A true believer is in a high degree protected against the danger of certain neurotic afflictions; by accepting the universal neurosis he is spared the task of forming a personal neurosis.

—Sigmund Freud

The word 'belief' is a difficult thing for me. I don't *believe*. I must have a reason for a certain hypothesis. Either I *know* a thing, and then I know it—I don't need to believe it.

—Carl Jung

Men who borrow their opinions can never repay their debts.

—Lord Halifax

With most men, unbelief in one thing springs from blind belief in another.

—Georg Christoph Lichtenberg

Many a time I have wanted to stop talking and find out what I really believed.

—Walter Lippman

The most positive men are the most credulous.

—Jonathan Swift

What a man thinks of himself, that it is which determines, or rather indicates, his fate.

—Henry David Thoreau

Betrayal

See also: Trust

It is all right to rat, but you can't re-rat.

—Winston Churchill

I hate the idea of causes, and if I had to choose between betraying my country and betraying my friend, I hope I should have the guts to betray my country.

—E. M. Forster

To betray, you must first belong. I never belonged.

—Kim Philby

Bible

See: Religion

If you believe what you like in the Gospel and reject what you do not like, it is not the Gospel you believe, but yourself.

—Augustine

Scriptures are the sacred books of our holy religion, as distinguished from the false and profane writings on which all other faiths are based.

—Ambrose Bierce

The Bible tells us to love our neighbours and also to love our enemies, probably because they are generally the same people.

—G. K. Chesterton

The Bible is a window in this prison of hope, through which we look into eternity,

—John Sullivan Dwight

Unless we form the habit of going to the Bible in bright moments as well as in trouble, we cannot fully respond to its consolations because we lack equilibrium between light and darkness.

—*Helen Keller*

To say nothing of its holiness or authority, the Bible contains more specimens of genius and taste than any other volume in existence.

—*Walter S. Landor*

The less the Bible is read, the more it's translated.

—*C. S. Lewis*

So far as I can remember, there is not one word in the Gospels in praise of intelligence.

—*Bertrand Russell*

Most people are bothered by those passages of Scripture they do not understand, but the passages that bother me are those I do understand.

—*Mark Twain*

Biography

A well-written Life is almost as rare as a well-spent one.

—*Thomas Carlyle*

There is properly no history; only biography.

—*Ralph Waldo Emerson*

There is no life that can be recaptured wholly; as it was. Which is to say that all biography is ultimately fiction.

—Bernard Malamud

Discretion is not the better part of biography.

—Lytton Strachey

Biography lends to death a new terror.

—Oscar Wilde

Birth

See also: Children and Childhood

The moment you're born you're done for.

—Arnold Bennett

Having a baby is like taking your lower lip and forcing it over your head.

—Carol Burnett

No one recovers from the disease of being born, a deadly wound if there ever was one.

—E. M. Cioran

If nature had arranged that husbands and wives should have children alternatively, there would never be more than three in a family.

—Laurence Housman

About the only thing we have left that actually discriminates in favor of the plain people is the stork.

—Kin Hubbard

To heir is human.

—Dolores E. McGuire

The Body

See also: Health

A healthy body is a guest chamber for the soul: a sick body is a prison.

—Francis Bacon

One's eyes are what one is, one's mouth what one becomes.

—John Galsworthy

Our body is a well-set clock, which keeps good time, but if it be too much or indiscreetly tampered with, the alarm runs out before the hour.

—Joseph Hall

A fat paunch never breeds fine thoughts.

—St. Jerome

The human body . . . indeed is like a ship; its bones being the stiff standing-rigging, and the sinews the small running ropes, that manage all the motions.

—Herman Melville

A human being is an ingenious assembly of portable plumbing.

—Christopher Morley

The abdomen is the reason why man does not easily take himself for a god.

—Friedrich Nietzsche

Happiness is beneficial for the body, but it is grief that develops the powers of the mind.

—Marcel Proust

I have said that the soul is not more than the body,
And I have said that the body is not more than the soul, and nothing, but God, is greater to one than one's self is.

—Walt Whitman

Boldness and Initiative

See also: Ambition; Self-Esteem; Courage

Boldness is ever blind, for it sees not dangers and inconveniences; whence it is bad in council though good in execution.

—Francis Bacon

Oliver Twist has asked for more.

—Charles Dickens

Fortune befriends the bold.

—John Dryden

If the creator had a purpose in equipping us with a neck, he surely meant us to stick it out.

—Arthur Koestler

Fools rush in where angels fear to tread.

—Alexander Pope

Books and Reading

See also: Arts: Poetry; Arts: Writing; Censorship

Some books are to be tasted; others swallowed; and some to be chewed and digested.

—Francis Bacon

The true university of these days is a collection of books.

—Thomas Carlyle

A book is the only immortality.

—Rufus Choate

A room without books is like a body without a soul.

—Cicero

Some books leave us free and some books make us free.

—Ralph Waldo Emerson

Dictionaries are like watches. The worst is better than none; the best cannot be expected to go quite true.

—Samuel Johnson

I am a part of all I have read.

—John Kieran

I have given up reading books; I find it takes my mind off myself.

—Oscar Levant

No book is really worth reading at the age of ten which is not equally, and often far more, worth reading at the age of fifty and beyond.

—C. S. Lewis

There are two kinds of books, those than no one reads and those that no one ought to read.

—H. L. Mencken

A good book is the precious life-blood of a master spirit, treasured up to a life beyond life.

—John Milton

Real books should be the offspring not of daylight and casual talk but of darkness and silence.

—Marcel Proust

A classic is something that everyone wants to have read and nobody wants to read.

—Mark Twain

Bravery

See: Courage

Brotherhood

See: Equality; Humanity and Human Nature; Race

Business

See also: America and Americans; Capitalism; Economy; Money; Work

Every crowd has a silver lining.

—P. T. Barnum

For the merchant, even honesty is a financial speculation.

—Charles Baudelaire

The successful business man sometimes makes his money by ability and experience; but he generally makes it by mistake.

—G. K. Chesterton

The chief business of the American people is business.

—Calvin Coolidge

America can no more survive and grow without big business than it can survive and grow without small business.

—Benjamin Franklin

Whatever is not nailed down is mine. Whatever I can pry loose is not nailed down.

—Collis P. Huntingdon

Commerce is the great civilizer. We exchange ideas when we exchange fabrics.

—Robert Ingersoll

One third of the people in the U.S. promote while the other two thirds provide.

—Will Rogers

There are two times in a man's life when he should not speculate: when he can't afford it, and when he can.

—Mark Twain

It is not the crook in modern business that we fear but the honest man who does not know what he is doing.

—*Owen D. Young*

C

Capitalism

See also: Business; Economy; Money; Wealth; Work

Capitalism and communism stand at opposite poles. Their essential difference is this: The communist, seeing the rich man and his fine home, says: "No man should have so much." The capitalist, seeing the same thing, says: "All men should have as much."

—*Phelps Adams*

The inherent vice of capitalism is the unequal sharing of blessings; the inherent virtue of socialism is the equal sharing of miseries.

—*Winston Churchill*

We are too mealy-mouthed. We fear the word "capitalism" is unpopular. So we talk about the "free enterprise" system and run to cover in the folds of the flag and talk about the American way of life.

—*Eric A. Johnston*

. . . militarism . . . is one of the chief bulwarks of capitalism, and the day that militarism is undermined, capitalism will fail.

—Helen Keller

Capitalists are no more capable of self-sacrifice than a man is capable of lifting himself up by his bootstraps.

—Vladimir Ilyich Lenin

Capital is that part of wealth which is devoted to obtaining further wealth.

—Alfred Marshall

As a matter of practical necessity, socialist democracy may eventually turn out to be more of a sham than capitalist democracy ever was.

—Joseph Alois Schumpeter

Cars

See: Technology

Cats

See also: Nature: Animals

I love cats because I enjoy my home; and little by little, they become its visible soul.

—Jean Cocteau

Those who'll play with cats must expect to be scratched.

—Miguel de Cervantes

Dogs come when they're called; cats take a message and get back to you.

—Missy Dizick

In a cat's eyes, all things belong to cats.

—English Proverb

If you want to be a psychological novelist and write about human beings, the best thing you can do is keep a pair of cats.

—Aldous Huxley

Cats are intended to teach us that not everything in nature has a function.

—Garrison Keillor

Cats are living adornments.

—Edwin Lent

No matter how much cats fight, there always seem to be plenty of kittens.

—Abraham Lincoln

The cat is mighty dignified until the dog comes by.

—Southern Folk Saying

One of the most striking differences between a cat and a lie is that a cat has only nine lives.

—Mark Twain

Censorship

See: Freedom of the Press

Change

See also: Progress

It's hard for me to get used to these changing times. I can remember when the air was clean and sex was dirty.

—George Burns

For good and evil, man is a free creative spirit. This produces the very queer world we live in, a world in continuous creation and therefore continuous change and insecurity.

—Joyce Cary

Well, I find that a change of nuisances is as good as a vacation.

—David Lloyd George

All change is not growth; all movement is not forward.

—Ellen Glasgow

There is a certain relief in change, even though it be from bad to worse; as I have found in traveling in a stagecoach, that it is often a comfort to shift one's position and be bruised in a new place.

—Washington Irving

Change is not progress.

—H. L. Mencken

The reasonable man adapts himself to the world; the unreasonable one persists in trying to adapt the world to himself. Therefore, all progress depends on the unreasonable man.

—George Bernard Shaw

Everyone thinks of changing the world, but no one thinks of changing himself.

—Leo Tolstoy

If you want to make enemies, try to change something.

—Woodrow Wilson

Character

Time wounds all heels.

—Jane Ace

We are born princes and the civilizing process makes us frogs.

—Eric Berne

Character is that which can do without success.

—Ralph Waldo Emerson

Being generous is inborn; being altruistic is a learned perversity.

—Robert Heinlein

The hardest thing is writing a recommendation for someone we know.

—Kin Hubbard

Every man has three characters: that which he shows, that which he has, and that which he thinks he has.

—Alphonse Karr

Champions take responsibility. When the ball is coming over the net, you can be sure I want the ball.

—*Billie Jean King*

You can't go around hoping that most people have sterling moral characters. The most you can hope for is that people will pretend that they do.

—*Fran Lebowitz*

Character is what you are in the dark.

—*Dwight Moody*

We judge ourselves by our motives and others by their actions.

—*Dwight Morrow*

You can tell a lot about a fellow's character by his way of eating jellybeans.

—*Ronald Reagan*

A fanatic is a man who redoubles his efforts after he has forgotten his aims.

—*George Santayana*

We can tell our values by looking at our checkbook stubs.

—*Gloria Steinem*

Charity

One of the serious obstacles to the improvement of our race is indiscriminate charity.

—*Andrew Carnegie*

We do not quite forgive a giver. The hand that feeds us is in some danger of being bitten.

—Ralph Waldo Emerson

Charity sees the need, not the cause.

—German proverb

Charity: a thing that begins at home, and usually stays there.

—Elbert Hubbard

As the purse is emptied, the heart is filled.

—Victor Hugo

He who waits to do a great deal of good at once, will never do anything.

—Samuel Johnson

A bone to the dog is not charity. Charity is the bone shared with the dog, when you are just as hungry as the dog.

—Jack London

Charity creates a multitude of sins.

—Oscar Wilde

Charm

See also: Grace

If you have it, you don't need to have anything else, and if you don't have it, it doesn't much matter what else you have.

—J. M. Barrie

The greatest mistake is trying to be more agreeable than you can be.

—*Walter Bagehot*

All charming people have something to conceal, usually their total dependence on the appreciation of others.

—*Cyril Connolly*

Nothing is so old as a dilapidated charm.

—*Emily Dickinson*

"Charm"—which means the power to effect work without employing brute force—is indispensable to women. Charm is a woman's strength just as strength is a man's charm.

—*Havelock Ellis*

There are charms made only for distant admiration.

—*Samuel Johnson*

There is no personal charm so great as the charm of a cheerful temperament.

—*Henry Van Dyke*

Charm is more than beauty.

—*Yiddish proverb*

Children and Childhood

See also: Family; Parents

If a child annoys you, quiet him by brushing his hair. If this doesn't work, use the other side of the brush on the other end of the child.

—*Anonymous*

You have to love your children unselfishly. That's hard. But it's the only way.

—*Barbara Bush*

When children appear, we justify all our weaknesses, compromises, snobberies, by saying: "It's for the children's sake."

—*Anton Chekhov*

A child is a curly, dimpled lunatic.

—*Ralph Waldo Emerson*

Pretty much all the honest truth telling there is in the world is done by children.

—*Oliver Wendell Holmes*

Children are our most valuable natural resource.

—*Herbert Hoover*

Don't take up a man's time talking about the smartness of your children; he wants to talk to you about the smartness of his children.

—*Ed Howe*

Childhood sometimes does pay a second visit to man; youth never.

—*Anna Jameson*

Children are a great comfort in your old age and they help you to reach it faster, too.

—Lionel Kaufmann

The real menace in dealing with a five-year-old is that in no time at all you begin to sound like a five-year-old.

—Jean Kerr

Truth, which is important to a scholar, has got to be concrete. And there is nothing more concrete than dealing with babies, burps and bottles, frogs and mud.

—Jeane J. Kirkpatrick

The secret of dealing successfully with a child is not to be its parent.

—Mell Lazarus

Even when freshly washed and relieved of all obvious confections, children tend to be sticky.

—Fran Lebowitz

Posterity is the patriotic name for grandchildren.

—Art Linkletter

The best way to keep children at home is to make the atmosphere pleasant and let the air out of the tires.

—Dorothy Parker

Before I got married, I had six theories about bringing up children; now I have six children and no theories.

—Lord Rochester

Making the decision to have a child—it's momentous. It is to decide forever to have your heart go walking around outside your body.

—Elizabeth Stone

If you want a baby, have a new one. Don't baby the old one.

—Jessamyn West

The best way to make children good is to make them happy.

—Oscar Wilde

Children begin by loving their parents; as they grow older they judge them; sometimes they forgive them.

—Oscar Wilde

Christ

See: Jesus Christ

Christianity

See also: Jesus Christ

People in general are equally horrified at hearing the Christian religion doubted, and at seeing it practiced.

—Samuel Butler

Christianity has not been tried and found wanting; it has been found difficult and left untried.

—*G. K. Chesterton*

Christians were never meant to be respectable.

—*Harry Emerson Fosdick*

If Christian nations were nations of Christians, there would be no wars.

—*Soame Jenyns*

Organized Christianity has probably done more to retard the ideals that were its founder's than any other agency in the world.

—*Richard Le Gallienne*

I believe in Christianity as I believe in the sun—not only because I see it, but because by it I see everything else.

—*C. S. Lewis*

Going to church doesn't make you a Christian any more than going to the garage makes you a car.

—*Laurence J. Peter*

Christianity is a battle, not a dream.

—*Wendell Phillips*

The trouble with some of us is that we have been inoculated with small doses of Christianity which keep us from catching the real thing.

—*Leslie Dixon Weatherhead*

Church

See: Religion

Civilization

See also: Progress

All civilization has from time to time become a thin crust over a volcano of revolution.

—Havelock Ellis

The true test of civilization is, not the census, nor the size of the cities, nor the crops, but the kind of man that the country turns out.

—Ralph Waldo Emerson

Is it progress if a cannibal uses a knife and fork?

—Stanislaus J. Lec

Civilization is, after all, but a coat of paint that washes away when the rain falls.

—Auguste Rodin

You can't say civilization isn't advancing: in every war, they kill you in a new way.

—Will Rogers

We live in a Newtonian world of Einsteinian physics ruled by Frankensteinian logic.

—Bertrand Russell

Civilization is a limitless multiplication of unnecessary necessities.

—Mark Twain

Human history becomes more and more a race between education and catastrophe.

—H. G. Wells

Anyone can be a barbarian; it requires a terrible effort to remain a civilized man.

—Leonard Sidney Woolf

Clergy
See: God; Religion

Clothes
See: Dress; Appearances; Style

Comedy
See: Humor

Communication
See: Language

Communism
See also: Economy; Revolution

A communist is like a crocodile; when it opens its mouth you cannot tell whether it is trying to smile or preparing to eat you up.

—Winston Churchill

Communism possesses a language which every people can understand—its elements are hunger, envy, and death.

—Heinrich Heine

Communism has never come to power in a country that was not disrupted by war or corruption, or both.

—John F. Kennedy

The theory of Communism may be summed up in one sentence: Abolish all private property.

—Karl Marx

I never agree with Communists or any other kind of kept men.

—H. L. Mencken

Communists are people who fancied that they had an unhappy childhood.

—Gertrude Stein

The crusade against Communism was even more imaginary than the spectre of Communism.

—A. J. P. Taylor

Confidence

See: Boldness and Initiative; Self-Esteem

Conscience

See also: Ethics

He who sacrifices his conscience to ambition burns a picture to obtain the ashes.

—Chinese proverb

Conscience—the only incorruptible thing about us.

—*Henry Fielding*

Conscience is a mother-in-law whose visit never ends.

—*H. L. Mencken*

Conscience is, in most men, an anticipation of the opinion of others.

—*Sir Henry Taylor*

Conscience and cowardice are really the same things.

—*Oscar Wilde*

Consistency

A foolish consistency is the hobgoblin of little minds, adored by little statesmen and philosophers and divines.

—*Ralph Waldo Emerson*

The only completely consistent people are the dead.

—*Aldous Huxley*

Consistency is the last refuge of the unimaginative.

—*Oscar Wilde*

Conversation

Conversation is the enemy of food and good wine.

—Alfred Hitchcock

Better to remain silent and to be thought a fool than to speak out and remove all doubt.

—Abraham Lincoln

If you haven't got anything nice to say about anybody, come sit next to me.

—Alice Roosevelt Longworth

Conversation would be vastly improved by the constant use of four simple words: I do not know.

—André Maurois

A good listener is not only popular everywhere, but after a while, he knows something.

—Wilson Mizner

Kind words can be short and easy to speak, but their echoes are truly endless.

—Mother Teresa

Wise men talk because they have something to say; fools, because they have to say something.

—Plato

I often quote myself: it adds spice to my conversation.

—George Bernard Shaw

He has occasional flashes of silence that make his conversation perfectly delightful.

—Sydney Smith

Show me someone who never gossips and I'll show you someone who isn't interested in people.

—Barbara Walters

If other people are going to talk, conversation becomes impossible.

—James McNeill Whistler

Country, The

See also: Nature

The lowest and vilest alleys of London do not present a more dreadful record of sin than does the smiling and beautiful countryside.

—Sir Arthur Conan Doyle

It is quiet here and restful and the air is delicious. There are gardens everywhere, nightingales sing in the gardens, and police spies lie in the bushes.

—Maxim Gorky

There's a little country in all of us, a little frontier.

—Louis L'Amour

The country has charms only for those not obliged to stay there.

—Edouard Manet

I have no relish for the country; it is a kind of healthy grave.

—Sydney Smith

Anybody can be good in the country. There are no temptations there.

—Oscar Wilde

Courage

See also: Boldness and Initiative; Fear

Living at risk is jumping off the cliff and building your wings on the way down.

—Ray Bradbury

Courage is almost a contradiction in terms: it mean a strong desire to live taking the form of readiness to die.

—G. K. Chesterton

Courage is grace under pressure.

—Ernest Hemingway

The greatest test of courage on earth is to bear defeat without losing heart.

—Robert Ingersoll

One man with courage makes a majority.

—Andrew Jackson

Courage is doing what you are afraid to do. There can be no courage unless you're scared.

—Eddie Rickenbacker

Courage is the fear of being thought a coward.

—*Horace Smith*

Courage is resistance to fear, mastery of fear—not absence of fear.

—*Mark Twain*

It is very easy to forgive others their mistakes. It takes more guts and gumption to forgive them for having witnessed your own.

—*Jessamyn West*

Creativity

See also: Arts

Don't think! Thinking is the enemy of creativity. It's self-conscious, and anything self-conscious is lousy. You can't try to do things; you simply must do them.

—*Ray Bradbury*

The merit of originality is not novelty; it is sincerity.

—*Thomas Carlyle*

All men are creative, but few are artists.

—*Paul Goodman*

Creativity can solve almost any problem. The creative act, the defeat of habit by originality overcomes everything.

—*George Lois*

Artists die twice. First creatively. Then physically. The second one is the easiest.

—Sylvester Stallone

Man was made at the end of the week's work when God was tired.

—Mark Twain

Crime

See also: Evil; Violence

Crimes, like virtues, are their own rewards.

—George Farquhar

Every once in a while, some feller without a single bad habit gets caught.

—Kin Hubbard

A thief believes everybody steals.

—Ed Howe

We don't seem to be able to check crime, so why not legalize it and then tax it out of business.

—Will Rogers

A criminal is a person with predatory instincts who has not sufficient capital to form a corporation.

—Howard Scott

Few men have virtue to withstand the highest bidder.

—George Washington

Criticism and Critics

See also: Advice

It was one of those plays in which the actors, unfortunately, enunciated very clearly.

—Robert Benchley

The covers of this book are too far apart.

—Ambrose Bierce

Blame is safer than praise.

—Ralph Waldo Emerson

To avoid criticism do nothing, say nothing, be nothing.

—Elbert Hubbard

Criticism is prejudice made plausible.

—H. L. Mencken

In all institutions from which the cold wind of open criticism is excluded, an innocent corruption begins to grow like a mushroom—for example, in senates and learned societies.

—Friedrich Wilhelm Nietzsche

Critics are a dissembling, dishonest, contemptible race of men. Asking a working writer what he thinks about critics is like asking a lamppost what it feels about dogs.

—John Osborne

This is not a novel to be tossed aside lightly. It should be thrown with great force.

—Dorothy Parker

A dramatic critic is a man who leaves no turn unstoned.

—George Bernard Shaw

I never give them hell; I just tell them the truth and they think it is hell.

—Harry S Truman

The public is the only critic whose opinion is worth anything at all.

—Mark Twain

Remember that nobody will ever get ahead of you as long as he is kicking you in the seat of the pants.

—Walter Winchell

Culture

Every man's ability may be strengthened or increased by culture.

—John Abbott

The acquiring of culture is the development of an avid hunger for knowledge and beauty.

—Jesse Bennett

Culture is one thing and varnish is another.

—Ralph Waldo Emerson

No culture can live, if it attempts to be exclusive.

—Mahatma Gandhi

One of the surest signs of the Philistine is his reverence for the superior tastes of those who put him down.

—Pauline Kael

Culture is the bedrock, the final wall, against which one leans one's back in a god-forsaken chaos.

—John Cowper Powys

Culture is the habit of being pleased with the best and knowing why.

—Henry Van Dyke

Culture is an instrument wielded by professors to manufacture professors, who, when their turn comes, will manufacture professors.

—Simone Weil

Custom

See also: Habit

The custom and fashion of today will be the awkwardness and outrage of tomorrow—so arbitrary are these transient laws.

—Alexandre Dumas

Custom is the plague of wise men and the idol of fools.

—Thomas Fuller

Men will sooner surrender their rights than their customs.

—Moritz Guedmann

Custom, then, is the great guide of human life.

—David Hume

Custom meets us at the cradle and leaves us only at the tomb.

—Robert Ingersoll

Have a place for everything and keep the thing somewhere else; this not advice, it is merely custom.

—Mark Twain

Cynics and Cynicism

A cynic is just a man who found out when he was ten that there wasn't any Santa Claus, and he's still upset.

—J. G. Cozzens

Cynicism is an unpleasant way of saying the truth.

—Lillian Hellman

A cynic is a man who, when he smells flowers, looks around for a coffin.

—H. L. Mencken

What is the use of straining after an amiable view of things, when a cynical view is most like to be the true one?

—George Bernard Shaw

A man who knows the price of everything and the value of nothing.

—Oscar Wilde

D

Dance

See: Arts: Music and Dance

Danger

See also: Trouble

Defend us from all perils and dangers of this night.

—*The Book of Common Prayer*

Of course I realized there was a measure of danger. Obviously I faced the possibility of not returning when first I considered going. Once faced and settled there really wasn't any good reason to refer to it.

—*Amelia Earhart*

As soon as there is life there is danger.

—*Ralph Waldo Emerson*

The most dangerous thing in the world is to try to leap a chasm in two jumps.

—*William Lloyd George*

The secret of reaping the greatest fruitfulness and the greatest enjoyment from life is to live dangerously!

—*Friedrich Neitzsche*

There is danger when a man throws his tongue into high gear before he gets his brain a-going.

—C. C. Phelps

A timid person is frightened before a danger, a coward during the time, and a courageous person afterwards.

—Jean Paul Richter

This country has come to feel the same when Congress is in session as when the baby gets hold of a hammer.

—Will Rogers

We cannot banish dangers, but we can banish fears. We must not demean life by standing in awe of death.

—David Sarnoff

Death

See also: Suicide

It's not that I'm afraid to die. I just don't want to be there when it happens.

—Woody Allen

There is a dignity in dying that doctors should not dare to deny.

—Anonymous

I do not believe that any man fears to be dead, but only the stroke of death.

—Francis Bacon

To die will be an awfully big adventure.

—J. M. Barrie

Now comes the mystery.

—Henry Ward Beecher

I am ready to meet my Maker. Whether my Maker is prepared for the ordeal of meeting me is another matter.

—Winston Churchill

Because I could not stop for Death,
He kindly stopped for me; The carriage held but just ourselves
And Immortality.

—Emily Dickinson

Death destroys a man, the idea of Death saves him.

—E. M. Forster

Sleep is lovely, death is better still, not to have been born is of course the miracle.

—Heinrich Heine

Teach me to live, that I may dread
The grave as little as my bed.

—Thomas Ken

The tombstone is about the only thing that can stand upright and lie on its face at the same time.

—Mary Wilson Little

Those who welcome death have only tried it from the ears up.

—Wilson Mizner

To fear love is to fear life, and those who fear life are already three parts dead.

—Bertrand Russell

Death seems to provide the minds of the Anglo-Saxon race with a greater fund of innocent amusement than any other single subject . . . the tale must be about dead bodies or very wicked people, preferably both, before the Tired Business Man can feel really happy.

—Dorothy L. Sayers

Death is more universal than life; everyone dies but not everyone lives.

—A. Sachs

All say, "how hard it is that we have to die"—a strange complaint to come from the mouths of people who have had to live.

—Mark Twain

Some people are so afraid to die that they never begin to live.

—Henry Van Dyke

Deception

The ring always believes that the finger lives for it.

—Chazal

You may be deceived if you trust too much, but you will live in torment if you do not trust enough.

—Frank Crane

The sure way to be cheated is to think one's self more cunning than others.

—François, Duc de La Rochefoucauld

It is double the pleasure to deceive the deceiver.

—Jean de la Fontaine

You can fool too many of the people too much of the time.

—James Thurber

When a person cannot deceive himself the chances are against his being able to deceive other people.

—Mark Twain

Deeds

See: Accomplishments; Work

Defeat

See: Victory

Democracy

See also: America and Americans; Equality; Freedom

Democracy means government by discussion, but it is only effective if you can stop people talking.

—Clement Atlee

In free countries, every man is entitled to express his opinions—and every other man is entitled not to listen.

—*G. Norman Collie*

Democracy becomes a government of bullies, tempered by editors.

—*Ralph Waldo Emerson*

Democracy is based up the conviction that there are extraordinary possibilities in ordinary people.

—*Harry Emerson Fosdick*

The job of a citizen is to keep his mouth open.

—*Günther Grass*

Democracy is the art of running the circus from the monkey cage.

—*H. L. Mencken*

Democracy substitutes election by the incompetent many for appointment by the corrupt few.

—*George Bernard Shaw*

It's not the voting that's democracy; it's the counting.

—*Tom Stoppard*

In Switzerland, they had brotherly love, five hundred years of democracy, and peace, and what did they produce: the cuckoo clock.

—*Orson Welles*

Democracy means simply the bludgeoning of the people by the people for the people.

—*Oscar Wilde*

Too many people expect wonders from democracy, when the most wonderful thing of all is just having it.

—*Walter Winchell*

Despair, Depression, Misery

When we are flat on our backs there is no way to look but up.

—*Roger W. Babson*

Facing it, always facing it, that's the way to get through. Face it.

—*Joseph Conrad*

What we call despair is often only the painful eagerness of unfed hope.

—*George Eliot*

Despair ruins some, presumption many.

—*Benjamin Franklin*

I am in that temper that if I were under water I would scarcely kick to come to the top.

—*John Keats*

The fact that God has prohibited despair gives misfortune the right to hope all things, and leaves hope free to dare all things.

—*Anne Sophie Swetchine*

Destiny

The mass of men lead lives of quiet desperation. What is called resignation is confirmed desperation . . . A stereotyped but unconscious despair is concealed even under what are called the games and amusements of mankind.

—Henry David Thoreau

Destiny

See: Fate

Dictators

See: Tyranny

Diet

. . . unnecessary dieting is because everything from television to fashion ads has made it seem wicked to cast a shadow. This wild emaciated look appeals to some women, though not to many men, who are seldom seen pinning up a *Vogue* illustration in a machine shop.

—Peg Bracken

Tell me what you eat, and I'll tell you what you are.

—Anthelme Brillat-Savarin

I've been on a diet for two weeks and all I've lost is two weeks.

—Totie Fields

As a child, my family's meal consisted of two choices; take it or leave it.

—Buddy Hackett

I feel about airplanes the way I feel about diets. It seems to me they are wonderful things for other people to go on.

—Jean Kerr

Diplomacy

Never answer a hypothetical question.

—Moshe Arens

A diplomat is a man who always remembers a woman's birthday but never remembers her age.

—Robert Frost

Diplomacy is to do and say the nastiest things in the nicest way.

—Isaac Goldberg

Diplomacy: Lying in state.

—Oliver Herford

Let us not negotiate out of fear, but let us never fear to negotiate.

—John F. Kennedy

A diplomat is one who can cut his neighbor's throat without his neighbor noticing it.

—Carlos P. Romulo

Diplomacy is the art of letting someone have your way.

—Daniele Vare

Discovery

See: Science

Divorce

I know one husband and wife who, whatever the official reasons given to the court for the breakup of their marriage, were really divorced because the husband believed that nobody ought to read while he was talking and the wife that nobody ought to talk while she was reading.

—Vera Brittain

The only solid and lasting peace between a man and his wife is, doubtless, a separation.

—Lord Chesterfield

He's the kind of man a woman would have to marry to get rid of.

—Mae West

Judges, as a class, display, in the matter of arranging alimony, that reckless generosity which is found only in men who are giving away someone else's cash.

—P. G. Wodehouse

Dogs

A dog is the only thing on this earth that loves you more than he loves himself.

—*Josh Billings*

The greatest pleasure of a dog is that you may make a fool of yourself with him, and not only will he not scold you, but he will make a fool of himself too.

—*Samuel Butler*

To his dog, every man is Napoleon; hence the constant popularity of dogs.

—*Aldous Huxley*

To be sure, the dog is loyal. But why, on that account, should we take him as an example? He is loyal to men, not to other dogs.

—*Karl Kraus*

Histories are more full of examples of fidelity of dogs than of friends.

—*Alexander Pope*

The more I see of men, the better I like dogs.

—*Mme. Roland*

The average dog is a nicer person than the average person.

—*Andrew A. Rooney*

If you pick up a starving dog and make him prosperous, he will not bite you. That is the principal difference between a dog and a man.

—*Mark Twain*

The dog has seldom been successful in pulling man up to its level of sagacity, but man has frequently dragged the dog down to his.

—*James Thurber*

A reasonable number of fleas is good for a dog, keeps him from brooding over being a dog.

—*Edward Westcott*

But was there ever a dog that praised his fleas?

—*W. B. Yeats*

Doing

See: Accomplishments; Virtue; Work

Doubt

See: Skepticism

Drama

See: Arts: Drama and Acting

Dreamers and Dreams

See also: Ambition; Psychology/Psychiatry; Vision

If one is lucky, a solitary fantasy can totally transform one million realities.

—*Maya Angelou*

Imagination is the highest kite one can fly.

—*Lauren Bacall*

. . . dreams are, by definition, cursed with short life spans.

—*Candice Bergen*

Dreaming permits each and every one of us to be quietly and safely insane every night of our lives.

—*Charles William Dement*

The end of wisdom is to dream high enough to lose the dream in the seeking of it.

—*William Faulkner*

I believe that dreams transport us through the underside of our days, and that if we wish to become acquainted with the dark side of what we are, the signposts are there, waiting for us to translate them.

—*Gail Godwin*

All men of action are dreamers.

—*James G. Huneker*

Keep true to the dreams of thy youth.

—*Johann von Schiller*

I was not looking for my dreams to interpret my life, but rather for my life to interpret my dreams.

—*Susan Sontag*

Reach high, for stars lie hidden in your soul. Dream deep, for every dream precedes the goal.

—Pamela Vaull Starr

Dress

See also: Appearance; Style

Keeping your clothes well pressed will keep you from looking hard pressed.

—Coleman Cox

Eat to please thyself, but dress to please others.

—Benjamin Franklin

Taking off my stays at the end of the day makes me happier than anything I know.

—Joyce Grenfell

The well-dressed man is he whose clothes you never notice.

—W. Somerset Maugham

If a woman rebels against high-heeled shoes, she should take care to do it in a very smart hat.

—George Bernard Shaw

I say, beware of all enterprises that require new clothes, and not rather a wearer of new clothes.

—Henry David Thoreau

She looked as though she had been poured into her clothes and had forgotten to say "when."

—P. G. Wodehouse

Drinking

See: Food and Eating

E

Earth

See also: Nature

Give me a firm place to stand, and I will move the earth.

—*Archimedes*

The earth is given as a common for men to labor and live in.

—*Thomas Jefferson*

The meek do not inherit the earth unless they are prepared to fight for their meekness.

—*H. J. Laski*

I don't know if there are men on the moon, but if there are they must be using the earth as their lunatic asylum.

—*George Bernard Shaw*

Earth fills her lap with pleasures of her own:
Yearnings she has in her own natural kind.

—*William Wordsworth*

Eating

See: Food and Eating

Economy

See also: Money

Economy is for the poor; the rich may dispense with it.

—*Christian Nestell Bovee*

Beware of little expenses; a small leak will sink a great ship.

—*Benjamin Franklin*

Only one fellow in ten thousand understands the currency question, and we meet him every day.

—*Kin Hubbard*

Every bright spot the White House finds in the economy is like the policeman bending over the body in the alley and saying cheerfully "Two wounds are fatal. The other one is not so bad."

—*John F. Kennedy*

Without economy none can be rich, and with it few will be poor.

—*Samuel Johnson*

If all economists were laid end to end, they would not reach a conclusion.

—*George Bernard Shaw*

Education

Education is the ability to listen to almost anything without losing your temper or self-confidence.

—*Anonymous*

Men get opinions as boys learn to spell,
By reiteration chiefly.

—*Elizabeth Barrett Browning*

When a subject becomes totally obsolete, we make it a required course.

—*Peter Drucker*

Only the educated are free.

—*Epictetus*

He who opens a school door, closes a prison.

—*Victor Hugo*

Education: the inculcation of the incomprehensible into the indifferent by the incompetent.

—*John Maynard Keynes*

Lack of education is an extraordinary handicap when one is being offensive.

—*Josephine Tey*

I have never let my schooling interfere with my education.

—*Mark Twain*

Education is an admirable thing, but nothing that is worth knowing can be taught.

—*Oscar Wilde*

Ego

See also: Vanity

He was like a cock who thought the sun had risen to hear him crow.

—George Eliot

He that falls in love with himself will have no rivals.

—Benjamin Franklin

When a man is wrapped up in himself, he makes a pretty small package.

—John Ruskin

Egotism—usually just a case of mistaken nonentity.

—Barbara Stanwyck

To love oneself is the beginning of a life-long romance.

—Oscar Wilde

Emotion

When dealing with people remember you are not dealing with creatures of logic, but with creatures of emotion, creatures bristling with prejudice, and motivated by pride and vanity.

—Dale Carnegie

Nothing is more injurious to the character and to the intellect than the suppression of generous emotion.

—John Joy Chapman

Half our mistakes in life arise from feeling where we ought to think, and thinking where we ought to feel.

—J. Churton Collins

The young man who has not wept is a savage, and the old man who will not laugh is a fool.

—George Santayana

It is easier to manufacture seven facts out of whole cloth than one emotion.

—Mark Twain

There is always something ridiculous about the emotions of people whom one has ceased to love.

—Oscar Wilde

Enemies

It is difficult to say who do you the most mischief: enemies with the worst intentions or friends with the best intentions.

—Edward Bulwer-Lytton

I will make you shorter by the head.

—Elizabeth I

Everyone needs a warm personal enemy or two to keep him free from rust in the movable parts of his mind.

—Gene Fowler

There is no little enemy.

—Benjamin Franklin

One should forgive one's enemies, but not before they are hanged.

—Heinrich Heine

If you have no enemies, you are apt to be in the same predicament in regard to friends.

—Elbert Hubbard

Scratch a lover, and find a foe.

—Dorothy Parker

A man cannot be too careful in the choice of his enemies.

—Oscar Wilde

Equality

Equality may perhaps be a right, but no power on earth can ever turn it into a fact.

—Honoré de Balzac

Equality is what does not exist among equals.

—e. e. cummings

There are many humorous things in the world: among them the white man's notion that he is less savage than the other savages.

—Mark Twain

Men are equal; it is not birth but virtue that makes the difference.

—Voltaire

Ethics

Ethics is about what is right, not who is right.

—Anonymous

Grub first, then ethics.

—Bertolt Brecht

Most people are willing to take the Sermon on the Mount as a flag to sail under, but few will use it as a rudder by which to steer.

—Oliver Wendell Holmes

What we might consider is how we are good rather than how good we are.

—Merrit Malloy

Evil

All that is necessary for the triumph of evil is that good men do nothing.

—Edmund Burke

The belief in a supernatural source of evil is not necessary; men alone are quite capable of every wickedness.

—Joseph Conrad

The lunatic's visions of horror are all drawn from the material of daily fact.

—William James

It is a sin to believe evil of others, but it is seldom a mistake.

—H. L. Mencken

Evil often triumphs, but never conquers.

—Joseph Roux

Even mother's milk nourishes murderers as well as heroes.

—George Bernard Shaw

I never wonder to see men wicked, but I often wonder to see them unashamed.

—Jonathan Swift

Between two evils, I always pick the one I never tried before.

—Mae West

Experience

Experience, which destroys innocence, also leads one back to it.

—James Baldwin

Experience is a school where a man learns what a big fool he has been.

—Josh Billings

If you know what you are doing, you can be daring.

—Gerald P. Finnerman

Technology . . . the knack of so arranging the world that we don't have to experience it.

—Max Frisch

Experience is not what happens to you. It is what you do with what happens to you.

—Aldous Huxley

Some luck lies in not getting what you thought you wanted but getting what you have, which, once you have got it, you may be smart enough to see is what you would have wanted had you known.

—Garrison Keillor

Experience is the name men give to their follies or their sorrows.

—Alfred De Musset

We learn from experience that men never learn anything from experience.

—George Bernard Shaw

When I was a boy of fourteen, my father was so ignorant I could hardly stand to have the old man around. But when I got to be twenty-one, I was astonished at how much the old man had learned in seven years.

—Mark Twain

Experience is simply the name we give our mistakes.

—Oscar Wilde

F

Failure

See also: Ambition; Boldness and Initiative; Despair, Depression, Misery

Ninety-nine percent of the failures come from people who have the habit of making excuses.

—*George Washington Carver*

Nothing fails like success.

—*G. K. Chesterton*

Show me a thoroughly satisfied man and I will show you a failure.

—*Thomas A. Edison*

He's no failure. He's not dead yet.

—*William Lloyd George*

Notice the difference between what happens when a man says to himself, "I have failed three times" and what happens when he says, "I am a failure."

—*S. I. Hayakawa*

Failure has no friends.

—*John F. Kennedy*

You don't die in the U.S., you underachieve.

—*Jerzy Kozinski*

No one is completely unhappy at the failure of his best friend.

—Groucho Marx

Faith

See also: Atheism; Belief; Fear; Religion

Faith is love taking the form of aspiration.

—William Ellery Channing

The greatest act of faith is when man decides he is not God.

—Oliver Wendell Holmes

Some things have to be believed to be seen.

—Ralph Hodgson

I always prefer to believe the best of everybody—it saves so much trouble.

—Rudyard Kipling

Faith may be defined briefly as an illogical belief in the occurrence of the improbable.

—H. L. Mencken

If a man have a strong faith he can indulge in the luxury of skepticism.

—Friedrich Nietzsche

Every human being is born without faith. Faith comes only through the process of making decisions to change before we can be sure it's the right move.

—Robert Schuller

Fame

Being a sex symbol is a heavy load to carry, especially when one is tired, hurt and bewildered.
—Clara Bow

Don't get excited over the noise you have made.
—Erasmus

If you would not be forgotten as soon as you are dead, either write things worth reading or do things worth writing about.
—Benjamin Franklin

Fame is so sweet that we love anything with which we connect it, even death.
—Blaise Pascal

Wealth is like sea-water; the more we drink, the thirstier we become and the same is true of fame.
—Arthur Schopenhauer

I stopped believing in Santa Claus when I was six. Mother took me to see him in a department store and he asked for my autograph.
—Shirley Temple

Even the best things are not equal to their fame.
—Henry David Thoreau

Fame is a vapor; popularity an accident; the only earthly certainty is oblivion.
—Mark Twain

Family

See also: Children and Childhood; Father; Mother; Parents

Happiness is having a large, loving, caring, close-knit family in another city.

—*George Burns*

There is probably nothing like living together for blinding people to each other.

—*Ivy Compton-Burnett*

Parenthood; that state of being better chaperoned than you were before marriage.

—*Marcelene Cox*

When I can no longer bear to think of the victims of broken homes, I begin to think of the victims of intact ones.

—*Peter De Vries*

Cleaning your house while your children are still growing is like shoveling the walk before it stops snowing.

—*Phyllis Diller*

A man finds out what is meant by a spitting image when he tries to feed cereal to his infant.

—*Imogene Fey*

The family is the ultimate American fascism.

—*Paul Goodman*

Families with babies and families without babies are sorry for each other.

—*Ed Howe*

In times of great stress, such as a four-day vacation, the thin veneer of family life wears off almost at once, and we are revealed in our true personalities.

—Shirley Jackson

The family you come from isn't as important as the family you're going to have.

—Ring Lardner

No matter how many communes anybody invents, the family always creeps back.

—Margaret Mead

Having a family is like having a bowling alley installed in your brain.

—Martin Mull

A family is unit composed not only of children but of men, women, and occasional animal, and the common cold.

—Ogden Nash

A man can't get rich if he takes proper care of his family.

—Navajo proverb

Happy families are all alike; every unhappy family is unhappy in its own way.

—Leo Tolstoy

Why pay money to have your family tree traced? Go into politics and your opponents will do it for you.

—Mark Twain

Fate

I do not believe in a fate that falls on men however they act, but I do believe in a fate that falls on men unless they act.

—G. K. Chesterton

We make our own fortunes and we call them fate.

—Benjamin Disraeli

When fate's got it in for you there's no limit to what you may have to put up with.

—Georgette Heyer

Lots of folks confuse management with destiny.

—Kin Hubbard

Do you know how helpless you feel if you have a full cup of coffee in your hand and you start to sneeze?

—Jean Kerr

Fate often puts all the material for happiness and prosperity into a man's hands just to see how miserable he can make himself.

—Don Marquis

Life is something that happens to you while you're making other plans.

—Margaret Millar

Father

See also: Family

I grew up to have my father's looks—my father's speech patterns—my father's posture—my father's walk—my father's opinions and my mother's contempt for my father.

—Jules Feiffer

The most important thing a father can do for his children is love their mother.

—Theodore Hesburgh

It's shattering to be told your father stinks.

—Julie Nixon

The fundamental defect of fathers is that they want their children to be a credit to them.

—Bertrand Russell

No man is responsible for his father. That is entirely his mother's affair.

—Margaret Turnbull

Fear

See also: Boldness and Initiative

The thing we run from is the thing we run to.

—Robert Anthony

Fear is created not by the world around us, but in the mind, by what we think is going to happen.

—Elizabeth Gawain

Fear of hypocrites and fools is the great plague of thinking and writing.

—Jules Gabriel Janin

The man who fears suffering is already suffering from what he fears.

—Michel de Montaigne

To conquer fear is the beginning of wisdom.

—Bertrand Russell

Whoever is abandoned by hope has also been abandoned by fear; this is the meaning of the word "desperate."

—Arthur Schopenhauer

To a man who is afraid, everything rustles.

—Sophocles

Feelings

See: Emotion

Fidelity

See: Loyalty

Flattery

Flattery is like cologne water, to be smelt of, not swallowed.

—Josh Billings

Flattery is from the teeth out. Sincere appreciation is from the heart out.

—Dale Carnegie

Flattery is counterfeit money which, but for vanity, would have no circulation.

—François, Duc de La Rochefoucauld

Just praise is a debt, but flattery is a present.

—Samuel Johnson

I hate careless flattery, the kind that exhausts you in your effort to believe it.

—Wilson Mizner

It is easy to flatter; it is harder to praise.

—Jean Paul Richter

Food and Eating

Few among those who go to restaurants realize the man who first opened one must have been a man of genius and a profound observer.

—Anthelme Brillat-Savarin

A good eater must be a good man; for a good eater must have a good digestion, and a good digestion depends upon a good conscience.

—Benjamin Disraeli

The bagel, an unsweetened doughnut with rigor mortis.

—Beatrice Freeman

All happiness depends on a leisurely breakfast.

—John Gunther

A man may be a pessimistic determinist before lunch and an optimistic believer in will's freedom after it.

—Aldous Huxley

Women never dine alone. When they dine alone they don't dine.

—Henry James

He was a bold man who first swallowed an oyster.

—King James I

Give me books, French wine, fruit, fine weather and a little music out of doors, played by somebody I do not know.

—John Keats

Civilized adults do not take apple juice with dinner.

—Fran Lebowitz

Large, naked, raw carrots are acceptable as food only to those who live in hutches eagerly awaiting Easter.

—Fran Lebowitz

All you see, I owe to spaghetti.

—Sophia Loren

To eat well in England you should have breakfast three times a day.

—W. Somerset Maugham

At a dinner party one should eat wisely but not too well, and talk well but not too wisely.

—*W. Somerset Maugham*

The art of dining well is no slight art, the pleasure not a slight pleasure.

—*Michel de Montaigne*

Fools and Foolishness

A fellow who is always declaring he's no fool, usually has his suspicions.

—*Anonymous*

The best way to convince a fool that he is wrong is to let him have his own way.

—*Josh Billings*

Let us be thankful for the fools. But for them, the rest of us could not succeed.

—*Robert Frost*

Fortune, seeing that she could not make fools wise, has made them lucky.

—*Michel de Montaigne*

Forgiveness

Forgive many things in others; nothing in yourself.

—*Ausonius*

There is no revenge so complete as forgiveness.

—Josh Billings

He who has not forgiven an enemy has not yet tasted one of the most sublime enjoyments of life.

—Johann Lavater

Always forgive your enemies—nothing annoys them so much.

—Oscar Wilde

Fortune

He that waits upon fortune, is never sure of a dinner.

—Benjamin Franklin

Fortune does not change men; it unmasks them.

—Suzanne Necker

Fortune knocks at every man's door once in a life, but in a good many cases the man is in a neighboring saloon and does not hear her.

—Mark Twain

Fraud

See: Deception; Honesty

Freedom

. . . everything can be taken from a man but one thing: the last of human freedoms—to choose one's attitude in any given set of circumstances—to choose one's own way.

—*Viktor Frankel*

When people are free to do as they please, they usually imitate each other.

—*Eric Hoffer*

We are not free; it was not intended we should be. A book of rules is placed in our cradle, and we never get rid of it until we reach our graves. Then we are free, and only then.

—*Ed Howe*

You are free and that is why you are lost.

—*Franz Kafka*

Freedom is indivisible, and when one man is enslaved, all are not free.

—*John F. Kennedy*

Freedom is only good as a means; it is no end in itself.

—*Herman Melville*

The only man who is really free is the one who can turn down an invitation to dinner without giving any excuse.

—Jules Renard

A hungry man is not a free man.

—Adlai Stevenson

Freedom of the Press

Only the suppressed word is dangerous.

—Ludwig Börne

Every burned book enlightens the world.

—Ralph Waldo Emerson

Our liberty depends on the freedom of the press, and that cannot be limited without being lost.

—Thomas Jefferson

Freedom of the press is limited to those who own one.

—A. J. Liebling

Friendship

Friendship is the finest balm for the pangs of despised love.

—Jane Austen

Think twice before you speak to a friend in need.

—Ambrose Bierce

A friend doesn't go on a diet because you are fat. A friend never defends a husband who gets his wife an electric skillet for her birthday. A friend will tell you she saw your old boyfriend—and he's a priest.

—Erma Bombeck

Santa Claus has the right idea: visit people once a year.

—Victor Borge

Intimacies between women often go backwards, beginning in revelations and ending in small talk.

—Elizabeth Bowen

The only thing your friends will never forgive you is your happiness.

—Albert Camus

My true friends have always given me that supreme proof of devotion, a spontaneous aversion for the man I loved.

—Colette

It is the friends you can call up at 4 a.m. that matter.

—Marlene Dietrich

We challenge one another to be funnier and smarter . . . It's the way friends make love to one another.

—Annie Gottlieb

If a man does not make new acquaintances as he advances through life, he will soon find himself left alone; one should keep his friendships in constant repair.

—Samuel Johnson

Friendship is a common belief in the same fallacies, mountebanks and hobgoblins.

—H. L. Mencken

If it's very painful for you to criticize your friends—you're safe in doing it. But if you take the slightest pleasure in it, that's the time to hold your tongue.

—Alice Duer Miller

True friendship is never serene.

—Marquise de Sévigné

The only safe and sure way to destroy an enemy is to make him your friend.

—Mark Twain

A real friend is one who walks in when the rest of the world walks out.

—Walter Winchell

I have lost friends, some by death . . . others by sheer inability to cross the street.

—Virginia Woolf

Future

The future is like heaven—everyone exalts it, but no one wants to go there now.

—James Baldwin

The future is an opaque mirror. Anyone who tries to look into it sees nothing but the dim outlines of an old worried face.

—Jim Bishop

I never think of the future; it comes soon enough.

—Albert Einstein

I like the dreams of the future better than the history of the past.

—Patrick Henry

We should all be concerned about the future because we will have to spend the rest of our lives there.

—Charles Kettering

It is bad enough to know the past; it would be intolerable to know the future.

—W. Somerset Maugham

If you want a picture of the future, imagine a boot stomping on a human face—forever.

—George Orwell

The trouble with our times is that the future is not what it used to be.

—Paul Valéry

G

Gambling

The gambling known as business looks with severe disfavor on the business known as gambling.

—*Ambrose Bierce*

Death and dice level all distinctions.

—*Samuel Foote*

Gambling promises the poor what property performs for the rich: that is why the bishops dare not denounce it fundamentally.

—*George Bernard Shaw*

It is the child of avarice, the brother of iniquity, and the father of mischief.

—*George Washington*

One should always play fairly when one has the winning cards.

—*Oscar Wilde*

Genius

The difference between genius and stupidity is that genius has its limits.

—*Anonymous*

One of the strongest characteristics of genius is the power of lighting its own fire.

—John Watson Foster

Genius without education is like silver in the mine.

—Benjamin Franklin

To mediocrity genius is unforgivable.

—Elbert Hubbard

Sometimes men come by the name of genius in the same way that certain insects come by the name of centipede—not because they have a hundred feet, but because most people can't count above fourteen.

—George Christoph Lichtenberg

Some people possess talent, others are possessed by it. When that happens, a talent becomes a curse.

—Rod Serling

When a true genius appears in the world you may know him by this sign: that all the dunces are in confederacy against him.

—Jonathan Swift

Everybody denies I am a genius—but nobody ever called me one!

—Orson Welles

Masterpieces are not single and solitary births; they are the outcome of many years of thinking in common, of thinking by the body of the people, so that the experience of the mass is behind the single voice.

—Virginia Woolf

Girls

See: Children and Childhood; Woman

God

See also: Religion

All things bright and beautiful,
All creatures great and small,
All things wise and wonderful,
The Lord God made them all.

—Cecil Frances Alexander

I look at the universe and I know there's an architect.

—Jack Anderson

I respect the idea of God too much to hold it responsible for a world as absurd as this one is.

—Georges Dumahel

Let us fear God and we shall cease to fear man.

—Mohandas K. Gandhi

God will forgive me; that's his business.

—Heinrich Heine

God doesn't make orange juice; God makes oranges.

—Jesse Jackson

You must believe in God, in spite of what the clergy say.

—Benjamin Jowett

Man considers the actions, but God weighs the intentions.

—Thomas à Kempis

Perhaps God is not dead; perhaps God is himself mad.

—R. D. Laing

God dwells wherever man lets him.

—Mendel of Kotzk

God is the immemorial refuge of the incompetent, the helpless, the miserable. They find not only sanctuary in His arms, but also a kind of superiority, soothing to their macerated egos; He will set them above their betters.

—H. L. Mencken

Live among men as if God beheld you; speak to God as if men were listening.

—Seneca

There are scores of thousands of human insects who are ready at a moment's notice to reveal the Will of God on every possible subject.

—George Bernard Shaw

God is a writer, and we are both heroes and the readers.

—Isaac Bashevis Singer

If you talk to God, you are praying; if God talks to you, you have schizophrenia.

—Thomas Szasz

He who knows about depth, knows about God.

—Paul Tillich

Satan hasn't a single salaried helper; the Opposition employs a million.

—Mark Twain

If God created us in his own image we have more than reciprocated.

—Voltaire

God gives himself to men as powerful or perfect. It is for them to choose.

—Simone Weil

Good

See also: Evil

The good die young—because they see it's no use living if you've got to be good.

—John Barrymore

No good deed goes unpunished.

—Clare Boothe Luce

On the whole human beings want to be good, but not too good and not quite all the time.

—George Orwell

If I knew for a certainty that a man was coming to my house with the conscious design of doing me good, I should run for my life.

—Henry David Thoreau

To be good, according to the vulgar standard of goodness, is obviously quite easy. It merely requires a certain amount of sordid terror, a certain lack of imaginative thought, and a certain low passion for middle-class respectability.

—Oscar Wilde

Gossip

Nobody's interested in sweetness and light.

—Hedda Hopper

There isn't much to be seen in a little town, but what you hear makes up for it.

—Kin Hubbard

The only time people dislike gossip is when you gossip about them.

—Will Rogers

I remember that a wise friend of mine did usually say, 'that which is everybody's business is nobody's business.'

—Izaak Walton

The only thing worse than being talked about is not being talked about.

—*Oscar Wilde*

Gossip is the art of saying nothing in a way that leaves practically nothing unsaid.

—*Walter Winchell*

Government

I believe our country is strong enough to be criticized.

—*Jack Anderson*

All free governments are managed by the combined wisdom and folly of the people.

—*James A. Garfield*

Society is produced by our wants and government by our wickedness.

—*Thomas Paine*

A government is the only known vessel that leaks from the top.

—*James Reston*

Grace

Beauty and grace command the world.

—*Park Benjamin*

How inimitably graceful children are before they learn to dance.

—*Samuel Taylor Coleridge*

Grace is to the body, what good sense is to the mind.

—François, Duc de La Rochefoucauld

Gratitude

Gratitude is not only the greatest of virtues, but the parent of all the others.

—Cicero

I feel a very unusual sensation—if it is not indigestion, I think it must be gratitude.

—Benjamin Disraeli

Gratitude is when memory is stored in the heart and not in the mind.

—Lionel Hampton

Greed
See: Selfishness

Grief

It is dangerous to abandon oneself to the luxury of grief: it deprives one of courage, and even of the wish for recovery.

—Henri Frédéric Amiel

Grief is so selfish.

—Mary Elizabeth Braddon

Let mourning stop when one's grief is fully expressed.

—Confucius

To live is to suffer, to survive is to find meaning in suffering.

—Viktor Frankel

Grief is a species of idleness.

—Samuel Johnson

There is a great deal of pain in life and perhaps the only pain that can be avoided is the pain that comes from trying to avoid pain.

—R. D. Laing

The only cure for grief is action.

—George Henry Lewes

Sorrow is so easy to express and yet so hard to tell.

—Joni Mitchell

Excess of grief for the deceased is madness, for it is an injury to the living, and the dead know it not.

—Xenophanes

Guilt
See: Crime

H

Habit

Chaos often breeds life, when order breeds habit.

—Henry Adams

Habit, if not resisted, soon becomes necessity.

—St. Augustine

Cultivate only the habits that you are willing should master you.

—Elbert Hubbard

The fixity of a habit is generally in direct proportion to its absurdity.

—Marcel Proust

Happiness

Happiness is good health and a bad memory.

—Ingrid Bergman

A happy life is one spent in learning, earning, and yearning.

—Lillian Gish

It's pretty hard to tell what does bring happiness. Poverty and wealth have both failed.

—Elbert Hubbard

The happiest people seem to be those who have no particular reason for being happy except that they are so.

—William Inge

Happiness is not a reward—it is a consequence. Suffering is not a punishment—it is a result.

—Robert Ingersoll

Happiness is not something you experience, it's something you remember.

—Oscar Levant

Most folks are about as happy as they make up their minds to be.

—Abraham Lincoln

The only really happy folk are married women and single men.

—H. L. Mencken

Men can only be happy when they do not assume that the object of life is happiness.

—George Orwell

Happiness is an imaginary condition, formerly attributed by the living to the dead, now usually attributed by adults to children, and by children to adults.

—Thomas Szasz

Hate

See also: Enemies

The more one is hated, I find, the happier one is.

—Louis-Ferdinand Céline

Hating people is like burning down your house to get rid of a rat.

—Harry Emerson Fosdick

It is better to be hated for what you are than to be loved for what you are not.

—André Gide

Now hatred is by far the longest pleasure;
Men love in haste, but they detest at leisure.

—Lord Byron

Like the greatest virtue and the worst dogs, the fiercest hatred is silent.

—Jean Paul Richter

I shall never permit myself to stoop so low as to hate any man.

—Booker T. Washington

Health

There's a lot of people in this world who spend so much time watching their health that they haven't the time to enjoy it.

—Josh Billings

The only thing harder to get rid of than a winter cold is a 1973 Ford Pinto.

—*Aileen Foster*

If you look like your passport photo, you're too ill to travel.

—*Will Kommen*

It's no longer a question of staying healthy. It's a question of finding a sickness you like.

—*Jackie Mason*

The only way to keep your health is to eat what you don't want, drink what you don't like, and do what you'd rather not.

—*Mark Twain*

The art of medicine consists of amusing the patient while nature cures the disease.

—*Voltaire*

One way to get high blood pressure is to go mountain climbing over molehills.

—*Earl Wilson*

Heaven

To believe in heaven is not to run away from life; it is to run toward it.

—*Joseph D. Blinco*

The few men who have managed to reach heaven must be terribly spoiled by this time.

—*Ed Howe*

If I have any beliefs about immortality, it is that certain dogs I have known will go to heaven, and very, very few persons.

—James Thurber

What a man misses mostly in heaven is company.

—Mark Twain

Hell

He did not think it was necessary to make a hell of this world to enjoy paradise in the next.

—William Beckford

When people no longer believe in hell, they promptly make this world into a place of torment.

—Edward Coleson

He should not preach about hell who cannot do it without tears.

—Dwight Moody

To be in hell is to drift; to be in heaven is to steer.

—George Bernard Shaw

History

All history is the propaganda of the victorious.

—Anonymous

Real solemn history, I cannot be interested in . . . The quarrels of popes and kings, with wars or pestilences in every page; the men all so good for nothing, and hardly any women at all.

—Jane Austen

The main thing is to make history, not to write it.

—Otto von Bismarck

History is a set of lies agreed upon.

Napoleon Bonaparte

God cannot alter the past, but historians can.

—Samuel Butler

There is no humorist like history.

—Will and Ariel Durant

Every major horror of history was committed in the name of an altruistic motive. Has any act of selfishness every equaled the carnage perpetuated by disciples of altruism?

—Ayn Rand

Those who cannot remember the past are condemned to repeat it.

—George Santayana

History is the ship carrying living memories into the future.

—Stephen Spender

On the whole history tends to be rather poor fiction—except at its best.

—Gore Vidal

Honesty

See also: Crime; Hypocrisy

If you attempt to beat a man down and so get his goods for less than a fair price, you are attempting to commit burglary as much as though you broke into his shop to take the things without paying for them. There is cheating on both sides of the counter, and generally less behind it than before.

—Henry Ward Beecher

Don't place too much confidence in the man who boasts of being as honest as the day is long. Wait until you meet him at night.

—Robert C. Edwards

Honesty pays, but it doesn't seem to pay enough to suit some people.

—Kin Hubbard

Men are able to trust one another, knowing the exact degree of dishonesty they are entitled to expect.

—Stephen Butler Leacock

It's better to be quotable than to be honest.

—Tom Stoppard

Hope

Hope is a good breakfast, but it is a bad supper.

—Francis Bacon

Second marriage: The triumph of hope over experience.

—Samuel Johnson

Hope in reality is the worst of all evils, because it prolongs the torments of man.

—Friedrich Nietzsche

A cathedral, a wave of a storm, a dancer's leap, never turn out to be as high as we had hoped.

—Marcel Proust

Honor begets honor; trust begets trust; faith begets faith, and hope is the mainspring of life.

—Henry L. Stimson

We are all in the gutter, but some of us are looking at the stars.

—Oscar Wilde

Humanity and Human Nature

There are times when you have to choose between being human and having good taste.

—Bertolt Brecht

Never appeal to a man's better nature. He may not have one. Invoking his self interest gives you more leverage.

—Robert Heinlein

We are what we pretend to be.

—Kurt Vonnegut, Jr.

I worry that humanity has been "advanced" to its present level of incompetency because evolution works on the Peter Principle.

—*Jane Wagner*

It's relaxing to go out with my ex-wife because she already knows I'm an idiot.

—*Thomas Warren*

Humor

Humor is the shortest distance between two people.

—*Victor Borge*

You can teach taste, editorial sense, but the ability to say something funny is something I've never been able to teach anyone.

—*Abe Burrows*

Start every day off with a smile and get it over with.

—*W. C. Fields*

Humor is an affirmation of dignity, a declaration to man's superiority to all that befalls him.

—*Romain Gary*

One doesn't have a sense of humor. It has you.

—*Larry Gelbart*

The sense of humor has other things to do than being conspicuous in the act of laughter.

—*Alice Meynell*

The absolute truth is the thing that makes people laugh.

—Carl Reiner

Humor is emotional chaos remembered in tranquility.

—James Thurber

Husbands

See also: Marriage; Men

It is easier to be a lover than a husband for the simple reason that it is more difficult to be witty every day than to produce the occasional bon mot.

—Honoré de Balzac

Husbands are awkward things to deal with; even keeping them in hot water will not make them tender.

—Mary Buckley

An archaeologist is the best husband a woman can have; the older she gets, the more interested he is in her.

—Agatha Christie

Intelligent women always marry fools.

—Anatole France

American husbands are the best in the world; no other husbands are so generous to their wives, or can be so easily divorced.

—Elinor Glyn

When you consider what a chance women have to poison their husbands, it's a wonder there isn't more of it done.

—Kin Hubbard

It is ridiculous to think you can spend your entire life with just one person. Three is about the right number. Yes, I imagine three husbands would do it.

—Clare Boothe Luce

Hypocrisy

I have seen hypocrisy that was so artful that it was good judgment to be deceived by it.

—Josh Billings

Man is the only animal that can remain on friendly terms with the victims he intends to eat.

—Samuel Butler

Clean your finger before you point at my spots.

—Benjamin Franklin

If it were not for the intellectual snobs who pay—in solid cash—the tribute which philistinism owes to culture, the arts would perish with their starving practitioners. Let us thank heaven for hypocrisy.

—Aldous Huxley

An ounce of hypocrisy is worth a pound of ambition.

—Michael Korda

The value of an idea has nothing to do with the success of the man who expresses it.

—Oscar Wilde

I

Ideals and Idealism

See also: Beliefs

Idealism is fine, but as it approaches reality the cost becomes prohibitive.

—William F. Buckley, Jr.

Idealism increases in direct proportion to one's distance from the problem.

—John Galsworthy

Words without actions are the assassins of idealism.

—Herbert Hoover

Idealism is the noble toga that political gentlemen drape over their will to power.

—Aldous Huxley

An idealist is one who, on noticing that a rose smells better than a cabbage, concludes that it will also make better soup.

—H. L. Mencken

Some men can live up to their loftiest ideals without ever going higher than a basement.

—Theodore Roosevelt

In our ideals we unwittingly reveal our vices.

—Jean Rostand

When they come down from their ivory towers, idealists are apt to walk straight into the gutter.

—Logan Pearsall Smith

Ideas

See also: Thought

The history of ideas is the history of the grudges of solitary men.

—E. M. Cioran

Ideas are the root of creation.

—Ernest Dimnet

Ideas must work through the brains and arms of men, or they are no better than dreams.

—Ralph Waldo Emerson

When they come, I write them, when they don't come, I don't.

—William Faulkner

To die for an idea is to set a rather high price on conjecture.

—Anatole France

There is one thing stronger than all the armies in the world, and that is an idea whose time has come.

—Victor Hugo

An idea that is not dangerous is unworthy of being called an idea at all.

—Don Marquis

The human mind treats a new idea the way the body treats a strange protein; it rejects it.

—P. B. Medawar

To die for an idea; it is unquestionably noble. But how much nobler it would be if men died for ideas that were true!

—H. L. Mencken

A powerful idea communicates some of its power to the man who contradicts it.

—Marcel Proust

We use ideas merely to justify our evil, and speech merely to conceal our ideas.

—Voltaire

Idleness

Work with some men is as besetting a sin as idleness with others.

—Samuel Butler

A loafer always has the correct time.

—Kin Hubbard

To be idle and to be poor have always been reproaches and therefore every man endeavors with his utmost care to hide his poverty from others and his idleness from himself.

—*Samuel Johnson*

Idleness is the stupidity of the body, and stupidity is the idleness of the mind.

—*Johann G. Seume*

To do nothing at all is the most difficult thing in the world, the most difficult and the most intellectual.

—*Oscar Wilde*

Ignorance

Ignorance gives one a large range of probabilities.

—*George Eliot*

There are many things of which a wise man might wish to be ignorant.

—*Ralph Waldo Emerson*

Ignorance is the necessary condition of life itself. If we knew everything, we could not endure existence for a single hour.

—*Anatole France*

He that knows little often repeats it.

—*Thomas Fuller*

He knows so little and knows it so fluently.

—*Ellen Glasgow*

Ignorance is the mother of all evils.
—Michel de Montaigne

If you are ignorant, you certainly can get into some interesting arguments.
—Herbert Prochnow

I do not approve of anything which tampers with natural ignorance.
—Oscar Wilde

Imagination

See also: Dreamers and Dreams; Vision

He who has imagination without learning has wings and no feet.
—Joseph Joubert

Without this playing with fantasy no creative work has every yet come to birth. The debt we owe to the play of imagination is incalculable.
—Carl Jung

You cannot depend on your eyes when your imagination is out of focus.
—Mark Twain

Imagination is a quality given a man to compensate him for what he is not, and a sense of humor was provided to console him for what he is.
—Oscar Wilde

Imitation

There is much difference between imitating a good man and counterfeiting him.

—Benjamin Franklin

No man ever yet became great by imitation.

—Samuel Johnson

To copy others is necessary, but to copy oneself is pathetic.

—Pablo Picasso

Insanity

Only the insane take themselves seriously.

—Max Beerbohm

Insanity destroys reason, but not wit.

—Nathaniel Emmons

Insanity: a perfectly rational adjustment to the insane world.

—R. D. Laing

When we remember we are all mad, the mysteries disappear and life stands explained.

—Mark Twain

Intelligence

See also: Knowledge; Wisdom

I would like to take you seriously but to do so would affront your intelligence.

—William F. Buckley, Jr.

A man is not necessarily intelligent because he has plenty of ideas any more than he is a good general because he has plenty of soldiers.

—*Nicolas Chamfort*

It is not enough to have a good mind. The main thing is to use it well.

—*René Descartes*

The test of a first-rate intelligence is the ability to hold two opposed ideas at the same time, and still retain the ability to function.

—*F. Scott Fitzgerald*

You cannot gauge the intelligence of an American by talking with him.

—*Eric Hoffer*

A moment's insight is sometimes worth a life's experience.

—*Oliver Wendell Holmes*

The voice of intelligence . . . is drowned out by the roar of fear . . . Most of all it is silenced by ignorance.

—*Karl Menninger*

The more intelligent one is, the more men of originality one finds. Ordinary people find no difference between men.

—*Blaise Pascal*

J

Jazz

See also: Music

Jazz is the only music in which the same note can be played night after night but differently each time.

—*Ornette Coleman*

Jazz will endure as long as people hear it through their feet instead of their brains.

—*John Philip Sousa*

Jazz is the folk music of the machine age.

—*Paul Whiteman*

Jealousy

Jealousy, the jaundice of the soul.

—*John Dryden*

Jealousy lives upon doubts. It becomes madness or ceases entirely as soon as we pass from doubt to certainty.

—*François, Duc de La Rochefoucauld*

The way to hold a husband is to keep him a little jealous; the way to lose him is to keep him a little more jealous.

—*H. L. Mencken*

And oft, my jealousy shapes faults that are not.
—William Shakespeare

Moral indignation is jealousy with a halo.
—H. G. Wells

Plain women are always jealous of their husbands, beautiful women never are. They are always so occupied with being jealous of other women's husbands.
—Oscar Wilde

Journalism

Never argue with people who buy ink by the barrel.
—Anonymous

Journalism is literature in a hurry.
—Matthew Arnold

A journalist is a grumbler, a censurer, a giver of advice, a regent of sovereigns, a tutor of nations. Four hostile newspapers are more to be feared than a thousand bayonets.
—Napoleon Bonaparte

Journalists do not live by words alone, although sometimes they have to eat them.
—Adlai Stevenson

Journalism is the ability to meet the challenge of filling space.
—Rebecca West

There is much to be said in favor of modern journalism. By giving us the opinions of the uneducated, it keeps us in touch with the ignorance of the community.

—Oscar Wilde

Joy

See: Happiness

Judgment

See also: Wisdom

It is well, when one is judging a friend, to remember that he is judging you with the same godlike and superior impartiality.

—Arnold Bennett

You shall judge of a man by his foes as well as by his friends.

—Joseph Conrad

The average man's judgment is so poor, he runs a risk every time he uses it.

—Ed Howe

We easily enough confess to others as to the advantage of courage, strength, experience, activity, and beauty, but an advantage in judgment we yield to none.

—Michel de Montaigne

Less judgment than wit is more sail than ballast.

—William Penn

We should all be obliged to appear before a board every five years and justify our existence on pain of liquidation.

—George Bernard Shaw

One cool judgment is worth a thousand hasty councils. The thing to do is to supply light and not heat.

—Woodrow Wilson

Justice

In the Halls of Justice the only justice is in the halls.

—Lenny Bruce

Whenever a separation is made between liberty and justice, neither, in my opinion, is safe.

—Edmund Burke

Children are innocent and love justice, while most adults are wicked and prefer mercy.

—G. K. Chesterton

Justice is always violent to the party offending, for every man is innocent in his own eyes.

—Daniel Defoe

The love of justice in most men is only the fear of themselves suffering by injustice.

—François, Duc de La Rochefoucauld

I find the public passion for justice quite boring and artificial, for neither life nor nature cares if justice is ever done or not.

—Patricia Highsmith

Justice is the insurance which we have on our lives and property. Obedience is the premium which we pay for it.

—William Penn

K

Killing

Kill one man and you are a murderer. Kill millions and you are a conqueror. Kill all and you are God.

—Jean Rostand

All creatures kill—there seems to be no exception. But of the whole list man is the only one that kills for fun; he is the only one that kills in malice, the only one that kills for revenge.

—Mark Twain

Kindness

Kindness is a language the dumb can speak and the deaf can hear and understand.

—*Christian Nestell Bovee*

You can get more with a kind word and a gun than you can get with a kind word alone.

—*Rachel Carson*

When kindness has left people, even for a few moments, we become afraid of them as if their reason has left them.

—*Willa Cather*

Forget injuries; never forget kindness.

—*Confucius*

If you're naturally kind, you attract a lot of people you don't like.

—*William Feather*

Wise sayings often fall on barren ground, but a kind word is never thrown away.

—*Sir Arthur Helps*

Kindness goes a long ways lots of times when it ought to stay at home.

—*Kin Hubbard*

He was so benevolent, so merciful a man that, in his mistaken passion, he would have held an umbrella over a duck in a shower of rain.

—*Douglas Jerrold*

To cultivate kindness is a valuable part of the business of life.

—*Samuel Johnson*

Kindness is loving people more than they deserve.

—*Joseph Joubert*

Not always actions show the man: we find,
Who does a kindness is not therefore kind.

—*Alexander Pope*

Human kindness has never weakened the stamina or softened the fiber of a free people. A nation does not have to be cruel in order to be tough.

—*Franklin D. Roosevelt*

One can always be kind to people about whom one cares nothing.

—*Oscar Wilde*

Kissing

God pardons like a mother who kisses the offense into everlasting forgetfulness.

—*Henry Ward Beecher*

A kiss is a lovely trick designed by nature to stop speech when words become superfluous.

—*Ingrid Bergman*

The sound of a kiss is not so loud as that of a cannon, but its echo last a great deal longer.

—*Oliver Wendell Holmes*

When women kiss, it always reminds me of prize fighters shaking hands.

—H. L. Mencken

A kiss can be a comma, a question mark or an exclamation point.

—Mistinguette

Marriage is the miracle that transforms the kiss from a pleasure into a duty.

—Helen Rowland

Soul meets soul on lover's lips.

—Percy Bysshe Shelley

Knowledge

See also: Books and Reading; Education

You can only have two things in life, reasons or results. Reasons don't count.

—Robert Anthony

Knowledge is power.

—Francis Bacon

To the small part of ignorance that we arrange and classify, we give the name knowledge.

—Ambrose Bierce

Knowledge is like money: the more he gets, the more he craves.

—Josh Billings

All that we know is, nothing can be known.

—Lord Bryon

Knowledge is knowing as little as possible.
—Charles Bukowski

I am always ready to learn although I do not always like being taught.
—Winston Churchill

Although it is dangerous to have too much knowledge of certain subjects, it is still more dangerous to be totally ignorant of them.
—Columbat

To know all is not to forgive all. It is to despise everybody.
—Quentin Crisp

As we acquire knowledge, things do not become more comprehensible, but more mysterious.
—Will Durant

Where is the life we have lost in living?
Where is the wisdom we have lost in knowledge?
Where is the knowledge we have lost in
information?
—T. S. Eliot

If a little knowledge is dangerous, where is the man who has so much as to be out of danger?
—Thomas Huxley

An extensive knowledge is needful to thinking people—it takes away the heat and fever; and helps, by widening speculation, to easy the Burden of the Mystery.
—John Keats

What a man knows is everywhere at war with what he wants.

—Joseph Wood Krutch

Letting people be okay without us is how we get to be okay without them.

—Merrit Malloy

The more unintelligent a man is, the less mysterious existence seems to him.

—Arthur Schopenhauer

A man is accepted into a church for what he believes and he is turned out for what he knows.

—Mark Twain

L

Labor

See also: Work

A man's best friends are his ten fingers.

—Robert Collyer

Labor is man's greatest function. He is nothing, he can do nothing, he can achieve nothing, he can fulfill nothing, without work.

—Orville Dewey

Excellence in any department can be attained only by the labor of a lifetime; it is not to be purchased at a lesser price.

—*Samuel Johnson*

It is only through labor and painful effort, by grim energy and resolute courage, that we move on to better things.

—*Theodore Roosevelt*

There is no real wealth but the labor of man.

—*Percy Bysshe Shelley*

Language

See also: Arts: Poetry and Poets; Arts: Writing; Books and Reading; Literature

Words have finished flirting; now they are making love.

—*André Breton*

The coldest word was once a glowing new metaphor.

—*Thomas Carlyle*

Language is the armory of the human mind, and at once contains the trophies of its past and the weapons of its future conquests.

—*Samuel Taylor Coleridge*

How can I tell what I think till I see what I say?

—*E. M. Forster*

The learned fool writes his nonsense in better language than the unlearned, but it is still nonsense.

—Benjamin Franklin

Language is the blood of the soul into which thoughts run and out of which they grow.

—Oliver Wendell Holmes

Think like a wise man but communicate in the language of the people.

—William Butler Yeats

Laughter

See also: Humor

Those who bring sunshine to the lives of others cannot keep it from themselves.

—James Matthew Barrie

He who laughs has not yet heard the bad news.

—Bertolt Brecht

Laughter is the tonic, the relief, the surcease for pain.

—Charlie Chaplin

If you don't learn to laugh at trouble, you won't have anything to laugh at when you're old.

—Ed Howe

Laughter is the sun that drives winter from the human face.

—Victor Hugo

I can usually judge a fellow by what he laughs at.

—*Wilson Mizner*

Wit has truth in it; wisecracking is simply calisthenics with words.

—*Dorothy Parker*

Comedy is simply a funny way of being serious.

—*Peter Ustinov*

Laughter is not at all a bad beginning for a friendship, and it is far the best ending for one.

—*Oscar Wilde*

Law

I learned law so well, the day I graduated I sued the college, won the case, and got my tuition back.

—*Fred Allen*

A law is valuable not because it is law, but because there is right in it.

—*Henry Ward Beecher*

The English laws punish vice; the Chinese laws do more; they reward virtue.

—*Oliver Goldsmith*

Laws that do not embody public opinion can never be enforced.

—*Elbert Hubbard*

The best way to get a bad law repealed is to enforce it strictly.

—Abraham Lincoln

The penalty for laughing in a courtroom is six months in jail; if it were not for this penalty, the jury would never hear the evidence.

—H. L. Mencken

You can't legislate intelligence and common sense into people.

—Will Rogers

The big print giveth and the small print taketh away.

—Bishop Fulton J. Sheen

Laws are like cobwebs, which may catch small flies but let wasps and hornets break through.

—Jonathan Swift

It is the spirit and not the form of law that keeps justice alive.

—Earl Warren

Leadership

The nation will find it very hard to look up to the leaders who are keeping their ears to the ground.

—Winston Churchill

Leadership: The art of getting someone else to do something you want done because he wants to do it.

—Dwight D. Eisenhower

In the great mass of our people there are plenty of individuals of intelligence from among whom leaders can be recruited.

—Herbert Hoover

The final test of a leader is that he leaves behind him in other men the conviction and the will to carry on.

—Walter Lippman

Learning

See also: Education; Teaching

There is no great concurrence between learning and wisdom.

—Francis Bacon

Wear your learning like your watch, in a private pocket, and do not pull it out and strike it merely to show that you have one.

—Lord Chesterfield

The University brings out all abilities, including stupidity.

—Anton Chekhov

The secret of education lies in respecting the pupil.

—Ralph Waldo Emerson

Learning makes a good man better and an ill man worse.

—Thomas Fuller

I've known countless people who were reservoirs of learning yet never had a thought.

—Wilson Mizner

Do you know the difference between education and experience? Education is when you read the fine print, experience is what you get when you don't.

—Pete Seeger

To be proud of learning is the greatest ignorance.

—Jeremy Taylor

We should live and learn; but by the time we've learned, it's too late to live.

—Carolyn Wells

Leisure

Also see: Idleness; Rest

Leisure is a beautiful garment, but it will not do for constant wear.

—Anonymous

The end of labor is to gain leisure.

—Aristotle

Leisure is the mother of philosophy.

—Thomas Hobbes

All intellectual improvement arises from leisure.
—Samuel Johnson

They talk of the dignity of work. Bosh. The dignity is in leisure.
—Herman Melville

To be able to fill leisure intelligently is the last product of civilization.
—Bertrand Russell

The secret of being miserable is to have the leisure to bother about whether you are happy or not.
—George Bernard Shaw

Liberty
Also see: Democracy; Justice

Absolute liberty is absence of restraint; responsibility is restraint; therefore, the ideally free individual is responsible to himself.
—Henry Brooks Adams

The God who gave us life gave us liberty at the same time.
—Thomas Jefferson

I believe in only one thing: Liberty; but I do not believe in liberty enough to want to force it upon anyone.
—H. L. Mencken

Liberty doesn't work as well in practice as it does in speeches.

—Will Rogers

Liberty means responsibility. That is why most men dread it.

—George Bernard Shaw

Liberty is the only thing you can't have unless you give it to others.

—William Allen White

Life

Life is not lost by dying; life is lost minute by minute, day by dragging day, in all the thousand small uncaring ways.

—Stephen Vincent Benét

Life is the childhood of our immortality.

—Goethe

It's hard to play Hamlet when you know the joke.

—Suzanna Cary

The art of life is to know how to enjoy a little and to endure much.

—William Hazlitt

You live and learn, or you don't live long.

—Robert Heinlein

Do not take life too seriously; you will never get out of it alive.

—Elbert Hubbard

The best use of life is to spend it for something that outlasts life.

—William James

Life is not the opposite of death, it is the absence of death.

—Merrit Malloy

The difference between life and the movies is that a script has to make sense, and life doesn't.

—Joseph L. Mankiewicz

Human existence is always irrational and often painful, but in the last analysis it remains interesting.

—H. L. Mencken

Life is not a spectacle or a feast; it is a predicament.

—George Santayana

Life does not cease being funny when people die any more than it ceases to be serious when people laugh.

—George Bernard Shaw

Life is a gamble at terrible odds. If it was a bet you wouldn't take it.

—Tom Stoppard

Life is like a B-grade movie. You don't want to leave in the middle of it, but you don't want to see it again.

—Ted Turner

Let us so live that when we come to die even the undertaker will be sorry.

—*Mark Twain*

Light

The pursuit of perfection, then, is the pursuit of sweetness and light.

—*Matthew Arnold*

Light is the first of painters. There is no object so foul that intense light will not make it beautiful.

—*Ralph Waldo Emerson*

There are two kinds of light—the glow that illumines, and the glare that obscures.

—*James Thurber*

Literature

Why do writers write? Because it isn't there.

—*Thomas Berger*

Literature is the art of writing something that will be read twice.

—*Cyril Connolly*

Only those things are beautiful which are inspired by madness and written by reason

—*André Gide*

The decline of literature indicates the decline of a nation.

—*Goethe*

A sequel is an admission that you've been reduced to imitating yourself.

—*Don Marquis*

Writing is the only profession where no one considers you ridiculous if you earn no money.

—*Jules Renard*

Literature: proclaiming in front of everyone what one is careful to conceal from one's immediate circle.

—*Jean Rostand*

Logic

See also: Reason; Science

If the world were a logical place, men would ride side-saddle.

—*Rita Mae Brown*

Logic, like whiskey, loses its beneficial effect when taken in too large quantities.

—*Lord Dunsany*

Men are apt to mistake the strength of their feeling for the strength of their argument. The heated mind resents the chill touch and relentless scrutiny of logic.

—*William E. Gladstone*

Logic: an instrument for bolstering a prejudice.

—*Elbert Hubbard*

Logic is neither a science nor an art, but a dodge.

—*Benjamin Jowett*

Logic is the art of going wrong with confidence.
—*Joseph Wood Krutch*

Loneliness

See also: Solitude

The eternal quest of the individual human being is to shatter his loneliness.
—*Norman Cousins*

In cities no one is quiet but many are lonely; in the country, people are quiet but few are lonely.
—*Geoffrey Francis Fisher*

If you are lonely while you're alone, you are in bad company.
—*Jean Paul Sartre*

Language has created the word "loneliness" to express the pain of being alone, and the word "solitude" to express the glory of being alone.
—*Paul Tillich*

The whole conviction of my life now rests upon the belief that loneliness, far from being a rare and curious phenomenon, peculiar to myself and to a few other solitary men, is the central and inevitable fact of human existence.
—*Thomas Wolfe*

Loss

See also: Grief

When wealth is lost, nothing is lost; when health is lost, something is lost; when character is lost, all is lost.

—German proverb

The cheerful loser is the winner.

—Elbert Hubbard

It's the good loser who finally loses out.

—Kin Hubbard

Wise men never sit and wail their loss, but cheerily seek how to redress their harms.

—William Shakespeare

Lose an hour in the morning, and you will spend all day looking for it.

—Richard Whately

Love

See also: Affection; Marriage; Husband; Wife; Passion

If there is anything better than to be loved it is loving.

—Anonymous

It is impossible to love and to be wise.

—Francis Bacon

The union of a want and a sentiment.

—Honoré de Balzac

Two minds without a single thought.

—Philip Barry

I never knew how to worship until I knew how to love.

—Henry Ward Beecher

Moved by a passion they do not understand for a goal they seldom reach, men and women are haunted by the vision of a distant possibility that refuses to be extinguished.

—Nathaniel Branden

I judge how much a man cares for a woman by the space he allots her under a jointly shared umbrella.

—Jimmy Cannon

Love is not entirely a delirium, yet it has many points in common therewith.

—Thomas Carlyle

When turkeys mate they think of swans.

—Johnny Carson

Love is the word used to label the sexual excitement of the young, the habituation of the middle-aged, and the mutual dependence of the old.

—John Ciardi

The art of love? It's knowing how to join the temperament of a vampire with the discretion of an anemone.

—E. M. Cioran

Tristan and Isolde were lucky to die when they did. They'd have been sick of all that rubbish in a year.

—Robertson Davies

The magic of first love is our ignorance that it can ever end.

—Benjamin Disraeli

Perhaps they were right in putting love into books . . . Perhaps it could not live anywhere else.

—William Faulkner

One is very crazy when in love.

—Sigmund Freud

The more you love someone the more he wants from you and the less you have to give since you've already given him your love.

—Nikki Giovanni

Love is a universal migraine,
A bright stain on the vision,
Blotting out reason.

—Robert Graves

Love's like the measles, all the worse when it comes late.

—Douglas Jerrold

Romantic love is a mental illness. But it's a pleasurable one. It's a drug. It distorts reality, and that's the point of it. It would be impossible to fall in love with someone that you really saw.

—Fran Lebowitz

A youth with his first cigar makes himself sick—a youth with his first girl makes other people sick.

—Mary Wilson Little

Love: the delusion that one woman differs from another.

—H. L. Mencken

Love is the triumph of imagination over intelligence.

—H. L. Mencken

The only abnormality is the incapacity to love.

—Anaïs Nin

In love there are two things—bodies and words.

—Joyce Carol Oates

By the time you swear you're his,
Shivering and sighing,
And he vows his passion is
Infinite, undying—
One of you is lying.

—Dorothy Parker

An attempt to change a piece of a dream-world into reality.

—Theodor Reik

Love is a canvas furnished by Nature and embroidered by imaginations.

—Voltaire

Women love men for their defects; if men have enough of them, women will forgive them everything, even their gigantic intellects.

—Oscar Wilde

Loyalty

See also: Patriotism

We join ourselves to no party that does not carry the American flag and keep step to the music of the Union.

—Rufus Choate

Unless you can find some sort of loyalty, you cannot find unity and peace in your active living.

—Josiah Royce

Loyalty means nothing unless it has at its heart the absolute principle of self-sacrifice

—Woodrow Wilson

Loyalty to petrified opinion never yet broke a chain or freed a human soul.

—Mark Twain

Luck

See also: Fate

As long as we are lucky we attribute it to our smartness; our bad luck we give the gods credit for.

—Josh Billings

It is the mark of an inexperienced man not to believe in luck.

—Joseph Conrad

Shallow men believe in luck. Strong men believe in cause and effect.

—Ralph Waldo Emerson

So unlucky that he runs into accidents which started out to happen to somebody else.

—Don Marquis

The only sure thing about luck is that it will change.

—Wilson Mizner

Chance favors the prepared mind.

—Louis Pasteur

Depend on the rabbit's foot if you will, but remember it didn't work for the rabbit.

—R. E. Shay

Luxury

Also see: Wealth

War destroys men, but luxury destroys mankind; at once corrupts the body and the mind.

—John Crowne

Possessions, outward success, publicity, luxury—to me these have always been contemptible. I believe that a simple and unassuming manner of life is best for every one, best for both the body and the mind.

—Albert Einstein

Give us the luxuries of life and we'll dispense with the necessaries.

—Oliver Wendell Holmes

Lying

See also: Deception

Never chase a lie. Let it alone, and it will run itself to death. I can work out a good character much faster than anyone can lie me out of it.

—Lyman Beecher

I do not mind lying, but I hate inaccuracy.

—Samuel Butler

There is no worse lie than a truth misunderstood by those who hear it.

—William James

Sin has many tools, but a lie is the handle that fits them all.

—*Oliver Wendell Holmes*

The truth that survives is simply the lie that is the pleasantest to believe.

—*H. L. Mencken*

M

Majority

See also: Democracy

Any man more right than his neighbors constitutes a majority of one.

—*Henry David Thoreau*

Whenever you find that you are on the side of the majority, it is time to reform.

—*Mark Twain*

It never troubles the wolf how many the sheep may be.

—*Virgil*

Man and Men

See also: Bachelors; Children and Childhood; Fathers; Husbands; Love; Marriage

I refuse to consign the whole male sex to the nursery. I insist on believing that some men are my equals.

—*Brigid Brophy*

Man is the only creature that refuses to be what he is.

—*Albert Camus*

The average man is more interested in a woman who is interested in him than he is in a woman with beautiful legs.

—*Marlene Dietrich*

Man is a reasoning rather than a reasonable animal.

—*Alexander Hamilton*

Man is the only animal that laughs and weeps; for he is the only animal that is struck with the difference between what things are, and what they ought to be.

—*William Hazlitt*

Men are more sentimental than women. It blurs their thinking.

—*Robert Heinlein*

It isn't the sissy men who help women most, but the rough, capable ones who can be caught and trained.

—Ed Howe

Man is simply the most formidable of all the beasts of prey, and indeed, the only one that preys systematically on its own species.

—William James

In all systems of theology the devil figures as a male person.

—Don Marquis

Man is a natural polygamist: he always has one woman leading him by the nose, and another hanging on to his coattails.

—H. L. Mencken

Men have a much better time of it than women; for one thing they marry later; for another thing, they die earlier.

—H. L. Mencken

Men are too emotional to vote. Their conduct at baseball games and political conventions shows this, while their innate tendency to appeal to force renders them particularly unfit for the task of government . . . Man's place is in the armory.

—Alice Duer Miller

I require three things in a man: he must be handsome, ruthless, and stupid.

—Dorothy Parker

Most men do not mature, they simply grow taller.

—Leo Rosten

A man's heart may have a secret sanctuary where only one woman may enter, but it is full of little anterooms which are seldom vacant.

—Helen Rowland

Every man sees a little of himself in Rhett Butler.

—Ted Turner

Man is a special being, and if left to himself, in an isolated condition, would be one of the weakest creatures; but associated with his kind, he works wonders.

—Daniel Webster

Man is a rational animal who always loses his temper when he is called upon to act in accordance with the dictates of reason.

—Oscar Wilde

Manners

See also: Behavior; Character

If a man be gracious, and courteous to strangers, it shows he is a citizen of the world . . .

—Francis Bacon

A man's own good breeding is the best security against other people's ill manners.

—Lord Chesterfield

Savages we call them because their manners differ from ours.

—Benjamin Franklin

The perfect hostess will see to it that the works of male and female authors be properly separated on her bookshelves. Their proximity, unless they happen to be married, should not be tolerated.

—Lady Gough's Etiquette (1836)

In society it is etiquette for ladies to have the best chairs and get handed things. In the home the reverse is the case. That is why ladies are more sociable than gentlemen.

—Virginia Graham

Manners easily and rapidly mature into morals.

—Horace Mann

The great secret is not having bad manners or good manners or any other particular sort of manners, but having the same manners for all human souls.

—George Bernard Shaw

For a man by no thing is so well betrayed,
As by his manners.

—Edmund Spenser

It is a mistake that there is no bath that will cure people's manners, but drowning would help.

—Mark Twain

To succeed in the world it is not enough to be stupid, you must also be well-mannered.

—Voltaire

Manners are especially the need of the plain. The pretty can get away with anything.

—Evelyn Waugh

Marriage

See also: Bachelors; Husbands; Love; Wife

Marriage is that relation between man and woman in which the independence is equal, the dependence mutual, and the obligation reciprocal.

—Louis K. Anspacher

Marriage is our last, best chance to grow up.

—Joseph Barth

Marriage is not just spiritual communion and passionate embraces; marriage is also three meals a day, sharing the workload and remembering to carry out the trash.

—Dr. Joyce Brothers

If you are afraid of loneliness, do not marry.

—Anton Chekhov

Marriage is an adventure, like going to war.

—G. K. Chesterton

Marriage is the aftermath of love.

—Noel Coward

The difficulty with marriage is that we fall in love with a personality, but must live with a character.

—Peter De Vries

It destroys one's nerves to be amiable every day to the same human being.

—Benjamin Disraeli

When there's marriage without love, there will be love without marriage.

—Benjamin Franklin

I don't think I'll get married again. I'll just find a woman I don't like and give her a house.

—Lewis Grizzard

Only choose in marriage a woman who you would choose as a friend if she were a man.

—Joseph Joubert

A successful marriage is an edifice that must be rebuilt every day.

—André Maurois

In a successful marriage, there is no such thing as one's way. There is only the way of both, only the bumpy, dusty, difficult, but always mutual path!

—Phyllis McGinley

A book of which the first chapter is written in poetry and the remaining chapters in prose.

—Beverly Nichols

Bad enough to make mistakes, without going ahead and marrying them.

—Craig Rice

It doesn't much signify whom one marries, for one is sure to find next morning that it was someone else.

—Samuel Rogers

Marriage is a bargain, and somebody has to get the worst of the bargain.

—Helen Rowland

Marriage resembles a pair of shears, so joined that they cannot be separated; often moving in opposite directions, yet always punishing any one who comes between them.

—Sydney Smith

By all means marry; if you get a good wife, you'll be happy. If you get a bad one, you'll become a philosopher.

—Socrates

One advantage of marriage, it seems to me, is that when you fall out of love with him, or he falls out of love with you, it keeps you together until you maybe fall in love again.

—Judith Viorst

Whenever you want to marry someone, go have lunch with his ex-wife.

—Shelley Winters

Maturity

The true test of maturity is not how old a person is but how he reacts to awakening in the mid-town area in his shorts.

—Woody Allen

Maturity is the time of your life when, if you had the time, you'd have the time of your life.

—Anonymous

Maturity is often more absurd than youth and very frequently is most unjust to youth.

—Thomas A. Edison

Growing up is after all only the understanding that one's unique and incredible experience is what everyone shares.

—Doris Lessing

The immature man wants to die nobly for a cause, while the mature man wants to live humanely for one.

—Wilhelm Stekel

One sign of maturity is knowing when to ask for help.

—Dennis Wholey

Medicine and the Medical Profession

The only profession that labors incessantly to destroy the reason for its own existence.

—James Bryce

Doctors are just the same as lawyers; the only difference is that lawyers merely rob you, whereas doctors rob you and kill you, too.

—Anton Chekhov

Never deny a diagnosis, but do deny the negative verdict that may go with it.

—Norman Cousins

God heals and the doctor takes the fee.

—Benjamin Franklin

A good deal of superciliousness
Is based on biliousness.
People seem as proud as peacocks
Of any infirmity, be it hives or dementia
praecox.

—Ogden Nash

We have not lost faith, but we have transferred it from God to the medical profession.

—George Bernard Shaw

Doctors are men who prescribe medicines of which they know little to cure diseases of which they know less, in human beings of whom they know nothing.

—Voltaire

Money

I'm tired of love, I'm still more tired of rhyme, but money gives me pleasure all the time.

—Hilaire Belloc

It is a kind of spiritual snobbery that makes people think they can be happy without money.

—*Albert Camus*

He that is of the opinion money will do everything may well be suspected of doing everything for money.

—*Benjamin Franklin*

The safest way to double your money is to fold it over once and put it in your pocket.

—*Kin Hubbard*

The richer your friends, the more they will cost you.

—*Elizabeth Marbury*

The two most beautiful words in the English language are "check enclosed."

—*Dorothy Parker*

But it is pretty to see what money will do.

—*Samuel Pepys*

Money is indeed the most important thing in the world; and all sound and successful personal and national morality should have this fact for its basis.

—*George Bernard Shaw*

Money is not required to buy one necessity of the soul.

—*Henry David Thoreau*

Virtue has never been as respectable as money.

—*Mark Twain*

When it is a question of money, everybody is of the same religion.

—Voltaire

Morality

The true meaning of religion is thus not simply morality, but morality touched by emotion.

—Matthew Arnold

About morals, I know only that what is moral is what you feel good after and what is immoral is what you feel bad after.

—Ernest Hemingway

Go into the street and give one man a lecture on morality and another a shilling, and see which will respect you most.

—Samuel Johnson

The one thing that doesn't abide by majority rule is a person's conscience.

—Harper Lee

Morality is the theory that every human act must be either right or wrong, and that 99 percent of them are wrong.

—H. L. Mencken

Morality is the best of all devices for leading mankind by the nose.

—Friedrich Nietzche

Never let your sense of morals interfere with doing the right thing.

—John Peer

Morality is the weakness of the mind.

—*Arthur Rimbaud*

All sects are different, because they come from men; morality is everywhere the same, because it comes from God.

—*Voltaire*

Morality is simply the attitude we adopt toward people whom we personally dislike.

—*Oscar Wilde*

Mothers

See also: Family; Father; Woman and Women; Wife

Any mother could perform the jobs of several air-traffic controllers with ease.

—*Lisa Alther*

I know how to do anything—I'm a mom.

—*Roseanne Barr*

A mother is neither cocky, nor proud, because she knows the school principal may call at any minute to report that her child had just driven a motorcycle through the gymnasium.

—*Mary Kay Blakely*

The mother's heart is the child's schoolroom.

—*Henry Ward Beecher*

A mother is not a person to lean on but a person to make leaning unnecessary.

—*Dorothy Canfield Fisher*

Mother is the dead heart of the family, spending father's earning on consumer goods to enhance the environment in which he eats, sleeps, and watches television.

—Germaine Greer

The only thing that seems eternal and natural in motherhood is ambivalence.

—Jane Lazarre

When you are a mother, you are never really alone in your thoughts. You are connected to your child and to all those who touch your lives. A mother always has to think twice, once for herself and once for her child.

—Sophia Loren

Most mothers are instinctive philosophers

—Harriet Beecher Stowe

Music

See: Arts: Music and Dance; Jazz

N

Name

See also: Character; Reputation

Nicknames stick to people, and the most ridiculous are the most adhesive.

—Thomas C. Haliburton

The invisible thing called a Good Name is made up of the breath of numbers that speak well of you.

—Lord Halifax

A nickname is the heaviest stone that the devil can throw at a man.

—William Hazlitt

A good name, like good will, is got by many actions and lost by one.

—Lord Jeffery

To live in mankind is far more than to live in a name.

—Vachel Lindsay

People of wealth and rank never use ugly names for ugly things.

—Sydney Smith

Nation

See also: America and Americans

A nation is a totality of men united through community of fate into a community of character.

—Otto Bauer

A nation never falls but by suicide.

—Ralph Waldo Emerson

Territory is but the body of a nation. The people who inhabit its hills and valleys are its soul, its spirit, its life.

—James A. Garfield

Nationalism

A nation is a thing that lives and acts like a man, and men are the particulars of which it is composed.

—Josiah G. Holland

No man has a right to fix the boundary of the march of a nation; no man has a right to say to his country—thus far shalt thou go and no farther.

—Charles Stewart Parnell

A nation, like a person, has a mind—a mind that must be kept informed and alert, that must know itself, that understands the hopes and needs of its neighbors—all the other nations that live within the narrowing circle of the world.

—Franklin D. Roosevelt

A nation that cannot preserve itself ought to die, and it will die—die in the grasp of the evils it is too feeble to overthrow.

—Morris Sheppard

Nationalism

See: Patriotism

Nature

Nature is a hanging judge.

—Anonymous

The ignorant man marvels at the exceptional; the wise man marvels at the common; the greatest wonder of all is the regularity of nature.

—George Dana Boardman

The imagination has no great task in portraying to itself a being removed from the everyday inducements to err which abound in civilized life, while he retains the best and simplest of his early impressions; who sees God in the forest, hears him in the winds; bows to him in the firmament that o'ercanopies all; submits to his sway in a humble belief of his justice and mercy—in a word, a being who finds the impress of the Deity in all the works of nature, without any of the blots produced by the expedients, and passion, and mistakes of man.

—James Fenimore Cooper

Civilization exists by geological consent, subject to change without notice.

—Will Durant

Nature encourages no looseness, pardons no errors.

—Ralph Waldo Emerson

Whatever Nature has in store for mankind, unpleasant as it may be, men must accept, for ignorance is never better than knowledge.

—Enrico Fermi

Nature does not complete things. She is chaotic. Man must finish, and he does so by making a garden and building a wall.

—Robert Frost

Though you drive away Nature with a pitchfork she always returns.

—Horace

In nature there are neither rewards nor punishments—there are consequences.

—Robert Ingersoll

There is nothing useless in nature; not even uselessness itself.

—Michel Montaigne

Man must go back to nature for information.

—Thomas Paine

Nature abhors a vacuum.

—François Rabelais

Whether man is disposed to yield to nature or to oppose her, he cannot do without a correct understanding of her language.

—Jean Rostand

Necessity

See also: Luxury; Wealth

Our necessities are few but our wants are endless.

—Josh Billings

Without death and decay, how could life go on?
—*John Burroughs*

We do what we must, and call it by the best names.
—*Ralph Waldo Emerson*

It is surprising what a man can do when he has to, and how little most men will do when they don't have to.
—*Walter Linn*

Necessity is the plea from every infringement of human freedom. It is the argument of tyrants; it is the creed of slaves.
—*William Pitt*

"Necessity is the mother of invention" is a silly proverb. "Necessity is the mother of futile dodges" is much nearer the truth.
—*A. N. Whitehead*

Neighbors
See also: Friendship

For what do we live, but to make sport for our neighbors, and laugh at them in our turn?
—*Jane Austen*

You're never quite sure how you feel about a neighbor until a "For Sale" sign suddenly appears in front of his house.
—*O. A. Battista*

It is discouraging to try to be a good neighbor in a bad neighborhood.

—William R. Castle

We make our friends; we make our enemies; but God makes our next-door neighbor.

—G. K. Chesterton

Love your neighbor, yet pull not down your hedge.

—George Herbert

Nothing makes you more tolerant of a neighbor's noisy party than being there.

—Franklin P. Jones

The crop always seems better in our neighbor's field and our neighbor's cow gives more milk.

—Ovid

What would I do without my neighbor when the grocery store is closed? One-fourth cup of sugar borrowed at a convenient time has saved many a pie, contributed to many a festivity.

—Dariel Walsh

Newspaper

See: Journalism

Nostalgia

Living in the past has one thing in its favor—it's cheaper.

—Anonymous

God gave us our memories so that we might have roses in December.

—*J. M. Barrie*

Reminiscence makes one feel so deliciously aged and sad.

—*George Bernard Shaw*

Nuclear Warfare
See: Technology; War

O

Obedience
See also: Children; Justice

Wicked men obey from fear; good men, from love.

—*Aristotle*

There are two kinds of men who never amount to much: those who cannot do what they are told, and those who can do nothing else.

—*Cyrus H. Curtis*

Obedience alone gives the right to command.

—*Ralph Waldo Emerson*

Those who know the least obey the best.

—*George Farquhar*

When a gentleman hath learned to obey he will grow very much fitter to command; his own memory will advise him not to command too rigorous punishments.

—Lord Halifax

The only safe ruler is he who has learned to obey willingly.

—Thomas à Kempis

Observation

See also: Science

Every man who observes vigilantly and resolves steadfastly grows unconsciously into genius.

—Edward G. Bulwer-Lytton

Each one sees what he carries in his heart.

—Goethe

We are very much what others think of us. The reception our observations meet with gives us courage to proceed, or damps our efforts.

—William Hazlitt

He alone is an acute observer, who can observe minutely without being observed.

—Johann K. Lavater

Opinion

See also: Belief; Ideas; Prejudice

I've always felt that a person's intelligence is directly reflected by the number of conflicting points of view he can entertain simultaneously on the same topic.

—Lisa Alther

The man who never alters his opinion is like standing water, and breeds reptiles of the mind.

—William Blake

The public buys its opinions as it buys its meat, or takes in its milk, on the principle that it is cheaper to do this than to keep a cow. So it is, but the milk is more likely to be watered.

—Samuel Butler

People do not seem to realize that their opinion of the world is also a confession of character.

—Ralph Waldo Emerson

Don't judge a man by his opinions, but by what his opinions have made him.

—Georg Christoph Lichtenberg

New opinions are always suspected, and usually opposed, without any other reason but because they are not already common.

—John Locke

The foolish and the dead alone never change their opinions.

—James Russell Lowell

Opinions cannot survive if one has no chance to fight for them.

—Thomas Mann

Opinion in good men is but knowledge in the making.

—John Milton

It's not that I don't have opinions, rather that I'm paid not to think aloud.

—Yitzhak Navon

Some praise at morning what they blame at night, But always think the last opinion right.

—Alexander Pope

It is clear that thought is not free if the profession of certain opinions makes it impossible to earn a living.

—Bertrand Russell

Opinion is something wherein I go about to give reason why all the world should think as I think.

—John Selden

Opinion is ultimately determined by the feelings, and not by the intellect.

—Herbert Spencer

Public opinion is a weak tyrant, compared with our private opinion—what a man thinks of himself, that is which determines, or rather indicates his fate.

—Henry David Thoreau

Opportunity

See also: Ability; Accomplishment/Achievement

A wise man will make more opportunities than he finds.

—Francis Bacon

Opportunity. A favorable occasion for grasping a disappointment.

—Ambrose Bierce

Occasions are rare; and those who know how to seize upon them are rarer.

—Josh Billings

You will never "find" time for anything. If you want time you must make it.

—Charles Buxton

Next to knowing when to seize an opportunity, the most important thing in life is to know when to forego an advantage.

—Benjamin Disraeli

No great man ever complains of want of opportunity.

—Ralph Waldo Emerson

You cannot make your opportunities concur with the opportunities of people whose incomes are ten times greater than yours.

—Edward S. Martin

Who seeks, and will not take when once 'tis
offer'd,
Shall never find it more.

—*William Shakespeare*

Oppression

See: Abuse; Tyranny

Optimism

See also: Pessimism

Optimist: a proponent of the doctrine that black is white.

—*Ambrose Bierce*

The optimist proclaims that we live in the best of all possible worlds; and the pessimist fears this is true.

—*James Branch Cabell*

The place where optimism flourishes most is the lunatic asylum.

—*Havelock Ellis*

Optimism is the content of small men in high places.

—*F. Scott Fitzgerald*

A pessimist is a man who has been compelled to live with an optimist.

—*Elbert G. Hubbard*

A cheerful resignation is always heroic, but no phase of life is so pathetic as a forced optimism.

—*Elbert Hubbard*

An optimist is a fellow who believes what's going to be will be postponed.

—*Kin Hubbard*

The habit of looking on the bright side of every event is worth more than a thousand pounds a year.

—*Samuel Johnson*

An optimist is a guy that has never had much experience.

—*Don Marquis*

The basis of optimism is sheer terror.

—*Oscar Wilde*

Originality

As soon as you can say what you think, and not what some other person has thought for you, you are on the way to being a remarkable man.

—*J. M. Barrie*

For I fear I have nothing original in me
Excepting Original Sin.

—*Thomas Campbell*

Originality is simply a pair of fresh eyes.

—*Thomas Wentworth Higginson*

All good things which exist are the fruits of originality.

—*John Stuart Mill*

Many a man fails as an original thinker simply because his memory is too good.

—*Friedrich Nietzsche*

The more intelligent a man is, the more originality he discovers in men. Ordinary people see no difference between men.

—*Blaise Pascal*

Originality does not consist in saying what no one has ever said before, but in saying exactly what you think yourself.

—*J. F. Stephen*

A man with a new idea is a crank until the idea succeeds.

—*Mark Twain*

Originality is nothing but judicious imitation.

—*Voltaire*

Ostentation

See: Pride

P

Pain

Man endures pain as an undeserved punishment; woman accepts it as a natural heritage.

—*Anonymous*

Pain dies quickly, and lets her weary prisoners go; the fiercest agonies have the shortest reign.

—*William Cullen Bryant*

Pain adds rest unto pleasure, and teaches the luxury of health.

—*Martin F. Tupper*

Parents

See also: Family; Father; Mother

Some people seem compelled by unkind fate to parental servitude for life. There is no form of penal servitude worse than this.

—*Samuel Butler*

The only people who seem to have nothing to do with the education of the children are the parents.

—G. K. Chesterton

There are times when parenthood seems nothing but feeding the mouth that bites you.

—Peter De Vries

How many hopes and fears, how many ardent wishes and anxious apprehensions are twisted together in the threads that connect the parent with the child.

—Samuel G. Goodrich

There must always be a struggle between a father and son, while one aims at power and the other at independence.

—Samuel Johnson

Greatness of name in the father oft-time overwhelms the son; they stand too near one another. The shadow kills the growth: so much that we see the grandchild come more and oftener to be the heir of the first.

—Ben Jonson

The best academy, a mother's knee.

—James Russell Lowell

Oh, what a tangled web do parents weave
When they think that their children are naive.

—Ogden Nash

I tell you there's a wall ten feet thick and ten miles high between parent and child.

—*George Bernard Shaw*

Fathers should be neither seen nor heard. That is the only proper basis for family life.

—*Oscar Wilde*

Passion

See also: Anger; Emotion

Passion is universal humanity. Without it religion, history, romance and art would be useless.

—*Honoré de Balzac*

The passions are like fire, useful in a thousand ways and dangerous only in one, through their excess.

—*Christian Nestell Bovee*

Passion, though a bad regulator, is a powerful spring.

—*Ralph Waldo Emerson*

Act nothing in furious passion. It's putting to sea in a storm.

—*Thomas Fuller*

The Past

The present contains nothing more than the past, and what is found in the effect was already in the cause.

—*Henri Bergson*

To look back to antiquity is one thing, to go back to it is another.

—Charles Caleb Colton

The past always looks better than it was; it's only pleasant because it isn't here.

—Finley Peter Dunne

The free world must now prove itself worthy of its own past.

—Dwight D. Eisenhower

Patience

Lord, grant me patience, and I want it right now.

—Anonymous

Patience: a minor form of despair, disguised as a virtue.

—Ambrose Bierce

Possess your soul with patience.

—John Dryden

Patience, that blending of moral courage with physical timidity.

—Thomas Hardy

Patience, the beggar's virtue.

—Philip Massinger

There is a point when patience ceases to be a virtue.

—Thomas Morton

Patriotism

See also: Nation

In time of war the loudest patriots are the greatest profiteers.

—*August Bebel*

In Dr. Johnson's famous dictionary, patriotism is defined as the last resort of a scoundrel. With all due respect to an enlightened but inferior lexicographer, I beg to submit that it is the first.

—*Ambrose Bierce*

When you hear a man speak of his love for his country, it is a sign that he expects to be paid for it.

—*H. L. Mencken*

Patriotism is the willingness to kill and be killed for trivial reasons.

—*Bertrand Russell*

Patriotism is a pernicious, psychopathic form of idiocy.

—*George Bernard Shaw*

Patriotism is the virtue of the vicious.

—*Oscar Wilde*

Peace

Peace: in international affairs, a period of cheating between two periods of fighting.

—*Ambrose Bierce*

What all men are really after is some form, or perhaps only some formula, of peace.

—Joseph Conrad

People in the long run are going to do more to promote peace than governments.

—Dwight D. Eisenhower

The most advantageous peace is better than the most just war.

—Erasmus

Anything for a quiet life.

—Thomas Heywood

If there is any peace it will come through being, not knowing.

—Henry Miller

Perseverance

Never give up: and never, under any circumstances, no matter what—never face the facts.

—Ruth Gordon

Concentrated effort along a single line of endeavor is boring, but it makes people rich.

—Lee Winkler

You do what you can for as long as you can, and when you finally can't, you do the next best thing. You back up but you don't give up.

—Chuck Yeager

Personality

See: Character

Pessimism

See also: Optimism; Skepticism

Pessimism is only the name that men of weak nerves give to wisdom.

—*Bernard De Voto*

Cheer up, the worst is yet to come.

—*Philander Johnson*

A pessimist is a person who has had to listen to too many optimists.

—*Don Marquis*

My pessimism extends to the point of even suspecting the sincerity of other pessimists.

—*Jean Rostand*

Pessimist: one who, when he has the choice of two evils, chooses both.

—*Oscar Wilde*

Philosophy

Philosophy: a route of many roads leading from nowhere to nothing.

—*Ambrose Bierce*

Those who lack the courage will always find a philosophy to justify it.

—*Albert Camus*

Philosophy is an unusually ingenious attempt to think fallaciously.

—Bertrand Russell

Philosophy teaches us to bear with equanimity the misfortunes of others.

—Oscar Wilde

Pity
See: Sympathy

Plagiarism
See also: Originality

About the most originality that any writer can hope to achieve honestly is to steal with good judgment.

—Josh Billings

Plagiarists are always suspicious of being stolen from.

—Samuel Taylor Coleridge

Plagiarists have, at least, the merit of preservation.

—Benjamin Disraeli

When you take stuff from one writer, it's plagiarism; but when you take it from many writers, it's research.

—Wilson Mizner

Pleasure

Pleasure is the absence of pain.

—Cicero

The honest man takes pains and then enjoys pleasures; the knave takes pleasure, and then suffers pain.

—Benjamin Franklin

A life of pleasure is the most unpleasant thing in the world.

—Oliver Goldsmith

The last pleasure in life is the sense of discharging our duty.

—William Hazlitt

I can sympathize with people's pains but not with their pleasures. There is something curiously boring about somebody else's happiness.

—Aldous Huxley

Pleasure is very seldom found where it is sought.

—Samuel Johnson

There is no such thing as pure pleasure; some anxiety always goes with it.

—Ovid

The true pleasure of life is to live with your inferiors.

—W. M. Thackeray

Simple pleasures are the last refuge of the complex.

—Oscar Wilde

All the things I really like to do are either immoral, illegal, or fattening.

—Alexander Woollcott

Poetry

See: Art: Poetry and Poets

Politics

See also: Government

Politics: the conduct of public affairs for private advantage.

—Ambrose Bierce

Anybody that wants the presidency so much that he'll spend two years organizing and campaigning for it is not to be trusted with the office.

—David Broder

Politics are too serious a matter to be left to the politicians.

—Charles De Gaulle

In politics there is no honor.

—Benjamin Disraeli

Politics is not the art of the possible. It consists in choosing between the disastrous and the unpalatable.

—John Kenneth Galbraith

You cannot adopt politics as a profession and remain honest.

—Louis McHenry Howe

The secret of the demagogue is to make himself as stupid as his audience so that they believe they are as clever as he.

—Karl Kraus

Being in politics is like being a football coach; you have to be smart enough to understand the game, and dumb enough to think it's important.

—Eugene McCarthy

The whole aim of practical politics is to keep the populace alarmed (and hence clamorous to be led to safety) by an endless series of hobgoblins.

—H. L. Mencken

One has to be a lowbrow, a bit of a murderer, to be a politician, ready and willing to see people sacrificed, slaughtered, for the sake of an idea, whether a good one or a bad one.

—Henry Miller

Politics is the diversion of trivial men who, when they succeed at it, become important in the eyes of more trivial men.

—George Jean Nathan

All politics are based on the indifference of the majority.

—James Reston

In politics if you want anything said, ask a man; if you want anything done, ask a woman.

—Margaret Thatcher

Popularity

See: Fame; Reputation

Poverty

There is no man so poor but what he can afford to keep one dog.

—Josh Billings

To be poor and independent is very nearly an impossibility.

—William Cobbett

Poverty is not a shame, but the being ashamed of it is.

—Thomas Fuller

Poverty is the openmouthed relentless hell which yawns beneath civilized society.

—Henry George

It's no disgrace t'be poor, but it might as well be.

—Kin Hubbard

The poor don't know that their function in life is to exercise our generosity.

—Jean Paul Sartre

We who are liberal and progressive know that the poor are our equals in every sense except that of being equal to us.

—*Lionel Trilling*

If the rich could hire other people to die for them, the poor could make a wonderful living.

—*Yiddish proverb*

Power

Power tends to corrupt and absolute power corrupts absolutely.

—*Lord Acton*

Power, like lightning, injures before its warning.

—*Calderón*

Power is the ability not to have to please.

—*Elizabeth Janeway*

Power is always gradually stealing away from the many to the few, because the few are more vigilant and consistent.

—*Samuel Johnson*

Wherever I found a living creature, there I found the will to power.

—*Friedrich Nietzsche*

The lust for power, for dominating others, inflames the heart more than any other passion.

—*Tacitus*

They who are in highest place, and have the most power, have the least liberty, because they are most observed.

—John Tillotson

Praise

See also: Flattery

Praises to the unworthy are felt by ardent minds as robberies of the deserving.

—Samuel Taylor Coleridge

Good men hate those who praise them if they praise them too much.

—Euripides

Our heartiest praise is usually reserved for our admirers.

—François, Duc de La Rochefoucauld

He that praiseth publickly, will slander privately.

—Thomas Fuller

Damn with faint praise, assent with civil leer. . . .

—Alexander Pope

Prayer

Pray: to ask the laws of the universe be annulled on behalf of a single petitioner confessedly unworthy.

—Ambrose Bierce

Certain thoughts are prayers. There are moments when, whatever be the attitude of the body, the soul is on its knees.

—Victor Hugo

The few words the better prayer.

—Martin Luther

Practical prayer is harder on the soles of your shoes than on the knees of your trousers.

—Austin O'Malley

Prejudice

If we were to wake up some morning and find that everyone was the same race, creed and color, we would find some other causes for prejudice by noon.

—George Aiken

A prejudice is a vagrant opinion without visible means of support.

—Ambrose Bierce

Prejudices are the props of civilization.

—André Gide

Prejudice is never easy unless it can pass itself off for reason.

—William Hazlitt

A great many people think they are thinking when they are merely rearranging their prejudices.

—William James

We must not allow prejudice to became a barrier to the full and effective use of our greatest national resources—the talents of our people.

—*Lynn A. Townsend*

Prejudice is the reasoning of the stupid.

—*Voltaire*

Passion and prejudice govern the world.

—*John Wesley*

I don't like principles. I prefer prejudices.

—*Oscar Wilde*

The Present

Those who live to the future must always appear selfish to those who live to the present.

—*Ralph Waldo Emerson*

The future is purchased by the present.

—*Samuel Johnson*

He to whom the present is the only thing that is present, knows nothing of the age in which he lives.

—*Oscar Wilde*

Pride

See also: Vanity

Excessive scruple is only hidden pride.

—*Johann Wolfgang von Goethe*

There was one who thought himself above me, and he was above me until he had that thought.

—Elbert Hubbard

Pride is seldom delicate; it will please itself with very mean advantages.

—Samuel Johnson

Pride is an admission of weakness; it secretly fears all competition and dreads all rivals.

—Fulton J. Sheen

The infinitely little have a pride infinitely great.

—Voltaire

Procrastination

Never do today what you can do tomorrow. Something may occur to make you regret your premature action.

—Aaron Burr

Procrastination is the art of keeping up with yesterday.

—Don Marquis

Never put off until tomorrow what you can do the day after tomorrow.

—Mark Twain

Procrastination is the thief of time.

—Edward Young

Progress

All progress is based upon a universal innate desire on the part of every organism to live beyond its income.

—Samuel Butler

What we call progress is the exchange of one nuisance for another nuisance.

—Havelock Ellis

Progress is the process whereby the human race is getting rid of whiskers, the veriform appendix, and God.

—H. L. Mencken

Not to go back is somewhat to advance, and men must walk, at least, before they dance.

—Alexander Pope

Providence

See: Fate

Psychology/Psychiatry

Neurotic means he is not as sensible as I am, and psychotic means that he is even worse than my brother-in-law.

—Karl Menninger

Life hardly ever lives up to our anxieties.

—Paul Monash

Why should I tolerate a perfect stranger at the bedside of my mind?

—Vladimir Nabokov

Psychiatry enables us to correct our faults by confessing our parents' shortcomings.

—Laurence J. Peter

Psychiatry is the care of the id by the odd.

—Unknown

The Public

One should respect public opinion insofar as is necessary to avoid starvation and keep out of prison, but anything that goes beyond this is voluntary submission to an unnecessary tyranny.

—Bertrand Russell

The public is a ferocious beast: one must either chain it up or flee from it.

—Voltaire

Punishment
See: Crime; Lying; Pain; Sin

Q

Quality
See also: Value

Everything to excess; every good quality is noxious if unmixed.

—*Ralph Waldo Emerson*

The best is the cheapest.

—*Benjamin Franklin*

It is the quality of our work which will please God and not the quantity.

—*Mahatma Gandhi*

Many individuals have, like uncut diamonds, shining qualities beneath a rough exterior.

—*Juvenal*

There is hardly anything in the world that some man cannot make a little worse and sell a little cheaper.

—*John Ruskin*

Quarrel

See also: Anger; Argument

People generally quarrel because they cannot argue.

—*G. K. Chesterton*

He that blows the coals in quarrels he has nothing to do with has no right to complain if the sparks fly in his face.

—*Benjamin Franklin*

Every quarrel begins in nothing and ends in a struggle for supremacy.

—*Elbert Hubbard*

Cut quarrels out of literature, and you will have very little history or drama or fiction or epic poetry left.

—*Robert Lynd*

When the chickens quit quarreling over their food they often find that there is enough for all of them. I wonder if it might not be the same with the human race.

—*Don Marquis*

Question

A prudent question is one-half of wisdom.

—*Francis Bacon*

A fool may ask more questions in an hour than a wise man can answer in seven years.

—*English proverb*

No question is so difficult to answer as that to which the answer is obvious.

—*George Bernard Shaw*

No man really becomes a fool until he stops asking questions.

—*Charles Steinmetz*

Judge a man by his questions rather than his answers.

—*Voltaire*

Quiet

See also: Rest; Silence

Quiet is what a home would be without children.

—*Anonymous*

An inability to stay quiet is one of the conspicuous failings of mankind.

—*Walter Bagehot*

The good and the wise lead quiet lives.

—*Euripides*

Very often the quiet fellow has said all he knows.

—*Kin Hubbard*

Quotation

You could compile the worst book in the world entirely out of selected passages from the best writers in the world.

—*G. K. Chesterton*

The wisdom of the wise and the experience of the ages are perpetuated by quotations.

—Benjamin Disraeli

He presents me with what is always an acceptable gift who brings me news of a great thought before unknown. He enriches me without impoverishing himself.

—Ralph Waldo Emerson

I often quote myself. It adds spice to my conversation.

—George Bernard Shaw

Now we sit through Shakespeare in order to recognize the quotations.

—Orson Welles

R

Race

See also: Prejudice

It is a great shock at the age of five or six to find that in a world of Gary Coopers you are the Indian.

—James Baldwin

The difference of race is one of the reasons why I fear war may always exist; because race implies difference, difference implies superiority, and superiority leads to predominance.

—Benjamin Disraeli

When white and black and brown and every other color decide they're going to live together as Christians, then and only then are we going to see an end to these troubles.

—Barry M. Goldwater

At the heart of racism is the religious assertion that God made a creative mistake when He brought some people into being.

—Friedrich Otto Hertz

Segregation is the adultery of an illicit intercourse between injustice and immorality.

—Martin Luther King

Mere connection with what is known as a superior race will not permanently carry an individual forward unless the individual has worth.

—Booker T. Washington

Reading

See also: Books and Reading; Literature

Reading is a basic tool in the living of a good life.

—Mortimer J. Adler

We should be as careful of the books we read, as of the company we keep. The dead very often have more power than the living.

—Tryon Edwards

Reading is like permitting a man to talk a long time, and refusing you the right to answer.

—Ed Howe

He has left off reading altogether, to the great improvement of his originality.

—Charles Lamb

Reading furnishes our mind only with materials of knowledge; it is thinking that makes what we read ours.

—John Locke

A man ought to read just as inclination leads him; for what he reads as a task will do him little good.

—Samuel Johnson

Reality

See also: Appearance, Dreams and Dreamers; Truth

My greatest enemy is reality. I have fought it successfully for thirty years.

—Margaret Anderson

Melancholy and remorse form the deep leaden keel which enables us to sail into the wind of reality.

—Cyril Connolly

Man . . . will debauch himself with ideas, he will reduce himself to a shadow if for only one second of his life he can close his eyes to the hideousness of reality.

—Henry Miller

Real life is, to most men, a long second-best, a perpetual compromise between the ideal and the possible.

—Bertrand Russell

The test which the mind applies to every question must be the test of reality; of validity measured through reason by reality. And yet the dogmatists call those weak who choose the harder, the more rigorous way.

—Dorothy Thompson

Reason

See also: Anger; Argument

As reason is a Revel unto Faith, so Passion unto Reason.

—Sir Thomas Browne

If you follow reason far enough it always leads to conclusions that are contrary to reason.

—Samuel Butler

He that will not reason is a bigot; he that cannot reason is a fool; and he that dares not reason is a slave.

—William Drummond

It's common for men to give pretended reasons instead of one real one.

—Benjamin Franklin

A man always has two reasons for doing anything—a good reason and the real reason.

—J. P. Morgan

The man who listens to Reason is lost; Reason enslaves all whose minds are not strong enough to master her.

—George Bernard Shaw

Rebellion

A populace never rebels from passion for attack, but from impatience of suffering.

—Edmund Burke

Men seldom, or rather never for a length of time and deliberately, rebel against anything that does not deserve rebelling against.

—Thomas Carlyle

An oppressed people are authorized when they can to rise and break their fetters.

—Henry Clay

As long as the world shall last there will be wrongs, and if no man objected and no man rebelled, those wrongs would last forever.

—Clarence Darrow

No one can go on being a rebel too long without turning into an autocrat.

—Lawrence Durrell

Religion

See also: Christianity

The true meaning of religion is thus not simply morality, but morality touched by emotion.

—Matthew Arnold

Religion is what keeps the poor from murdering the rich.

—Napoleon Bonaparte

Most religions do not make men better, only warier.

—Elias Canetti

It is the test of a good religion whether you can joke about it.

—G. K. Chesterton

Many have quarreled about religion that never practiced it.

—Benjamin Franklin

Religion is a monumental chapter in the history of human egotism.

—William James

Religion's in the heart, not in the knees.

—Douglas Jerrold

We have just enough religion to make us hate, but not enough to make us love one another.

—*Jonathan Swift*

Religion is the fashionable substitute for belief.

—*Oscar Wilde*

Reputation

See also: Character; Fame

The easiest way to get a reputation is to go outside the fold, shout around for a few years as a violent atheist or a dangerous radical, and then crawl back to the shelter.

—*F. Scott Fitzgerald*

What people say behind your back is your standing in the community.

—*Ed Howe*

He that hath the name to be an early riser may sleep till noon.

—*James Howell*

Many a man's reputation would not know his character if they met on the street.

—*Elbert Hubbard*

Perhaps the most valuable of all human possessions, next to an aloof and sniffish air, is the reputation of being well-to-do.

—*H. L. Mencken*

Associate with men of good quality if you esteem your own reputation; for it is better to be alone than in bad company.

—George Washington

Responsibility

Responsibility is the price of greatness.

—Winston Churchill

Responsibility is the thing people dread most of all. Yet it is the one thing in the world that develops us, gives us manhood or womanhood fibre.

—Frank Crane

You will find men who want to be carried on the shoulders of others, who think that the world owes them a living. They don't seem to see that we must all lift together and pull together.

—Henry Ford II

Rest

He that can take rest is greater than he that can take cities.

—Benjamin Franklin

Who remembers when we used to rest on Sunday instead of Monday?

—Kin Hubbard

Eternal rest sounds comforting in the pulpit; well, you try it once, and see how heavy time will hang on your hands.

—Mark Twain

Rest is a good thing, but boredom is its brother.

—Voltaire

Revenge

See: Hate; Vengeance

Revolution

See also: Government; Rebellion

Revolutions are not trifles, but spring from trifles.

—Aristotle

A revolution is interesting insofar as it avoids like the plague the plague it promised to heal.

—Daniel Berrigan

Make revolution a parent of settlement, and not a nursery of future revolutions.

—Edmund Burke

Revolutions are not made by men in spectacles.

—Oliver Wendell Holmes

Every revolution evaporates and leaves behind only the slime of a new bureaucracy.

—Franz Kafka

Those who make peaceful revolution impossible will make violent revolution inevitable.

—John F. Kennedy

Revolution is a trivial shift in the emphasis of suffering.

—Tom Stoppard

Reward

See also: Accomplishment/Achievement; Ambition; Success

The reward of a thing well done is to have done it.

—Ralph Waldo Emerson

He that does good for good's sake seeks neither paradise nor reward, but he is sure of both in the end.

—William Penn

Not in rewards, but in the strength to strive, the blessing lies.

—J. T. Towbridge

No man, who continues to add something to the material, intellectual and moral well-being of the place in which he lives is left long without proper reward.

—Booker T. Washington

Rights

Many a person seems to think it isn't enough for the government to guarantee him the pursuit of happiness. He insists it also run interference for him.

—Anonymous

This is the grave of Mike O'Day
Who died maintaining his right of way.
His right was clear, his will was strong.
But he's just as dead as if he'd been wrong.

—Anonymous

I am the inferior of any man whose rights I trample under foot.

—Robert Ingersoll

In giving rights to others which belong to them, we give rights to ourselves and to our country.

—John F. Kennedy

No man was ever endowed with a right without being at the same time saddled with a responsibility.

—Gerald W. Johnson

Always do right; this will gratify some people and astonish the rest.

—Mark Twain

S

Sacrifice

In this world it is not what we take up, but what we give up, that makes us rich.

—Henry Ward Beecher

They never fail who die in a great cause.

—Lord Byron

Good manners are made up of petty sacrifices.

—Ralph Waldo Emerson

The mice which helplessly find themselves between the cats' teeth acquire no merit from their enforced sacrifice.

—Mahatma Gandhi

We can offer up much in the large, but to make sacrifices in the little things is what we are seldom equal to.

—Goethe

It is a trick among the dishonest to offer sacrifices that are not needed, or not possible, to avoid making those that are required.

—I. A. Goncharov

The two things that worthless people sacrifice everything for are happiness and freedom, and their punishment is that they got both only to find that they have no capacity for the happiness and no use for the freedom.

—George Bernard Shaw

Safety

"Safety first" does not mean a smug self-satisfaction with everything as it is. It is a warning to all persons who are going to cross a road in dangerous circumstances.

—Stanley Baldwin

In skating over thin ice our safety is in our speed.

—Ralph Waldo Emerson

He that's secure is not safe.

—Benjamin Franklin

Try breaking into your own home. Most people find several ways to get inside in just a few minutes.

—Ray Johnson, former burglar

My definition of a free society is a society where it is safe to be unpopular.

—Adlai Stevenson

There is no safety in numbers, or in anything else.

—James Thurber

Salvation

He who created us without our help will not save us without our consent.

—Saint Augustine

No one can be redeemed by another. No God and no saint is able to shield a man from the consequence of his evil doings. Every one of us must become his own redeemer.

—Subhadra Bhikshu

The Christian is in a similar position to a sailor who has fallen overboard, has caught a line thrown to him by his mates, and is being pulled through the water to the safety of his ship. He can say, "I was saved when they threw me the line." He can also say, "I am being saved as they pull me through the water." And he can say, "I will be saved when I stand again on the deck of the ship."

—Carl Bridge, Jr.

Human salvation lies in the hands of the creatively maladjusted.

—Martin Luther King, Jr.

I was twenty years old before I ever heard a sermon on regeneration. I was always told to be good, but you might as well tell a midget to be a giant as to tell him to be good without telling him how.

—Dwight L. Moody

The salvation of the world depends on the men who will not take evil good-humouredly, and whose laughter destroys the fool instead of encouraging him.

—George Bernard Shaw

Scandal

A stink is still worse for the stirring.

—Miguel de Cervantes

Many of the scandals that I have seen have begun from glossing over unpleasant facts.

—Lord Chandos

Scandal is what one half of the world takes pleasure inventing, and the other half in believing.

—Paul Chatfield

Everybody says it, and what everybody says must be true.

—James Fenimore Cooper

The object of the scandalmonger is not that she tells of racy doings, but that she pretends to be indignant about them.

—H. L. Mencken

The malice of a good thing is the bar that makes it stick.

—Richard B. Sheridan

Gossip is charming! History is merely gossip. But scandal is gossip made tedious by morality.

—Oscar Wilde

Science

The laws of biology are the fundamental lessons of history.

—Will and Ariel Durant

Every great advance in science has issued from a new audacity of imagination.

—John Dewey

It stands to the everlasting credit of science that by acting on the human mind, it has overcome man's insecurity before himself and before nature.

—Albert Einstein

Most "scientists" are bottlewashers and button sorters.

—Robert Heinlein

Science is simply common sense at its best—that is, rigidly accurate in observation, and merciless to fallacy in logic.

—Thomas Huxley

Creativity in science could be described as the act of putting two and two together to make five.

—Arthur Koestler

There are no such things as applied sciences, only applications of science.

—Louis Pasteur

The universe is full of magical things, patiently waiting for our wits to grow sharper.

—Eden Phillpotts

Science is organized knowledge.

—Herbert Spencer

The science of today is the technology of tomorrow.

—Edward Teller

The secret of science is to ask the right question, and it is the choice of problem more than anything else that marks the man of genius in the scientific world.

—Sir Henry Tizard

It will free man from his remaining chains, the chains of gravity which still tie him to this planet. It will open to him the gates of heaven.

—Werner von Braun

Secrets and Secrecy

Two things a man cannot hide: that he is drunk, and that he is in love.

—Antiphanes

How can we expect someone else to keep our secret if we have not been able to keep it ourselves?

—François, Duc de La Rochefoucauld

Three may keep a secret if two of them are dead.

—Benjamin Franklin

Never tell a secret to a bride or a groom; wait until they have been married longer.

—Ed Howe

Secrets are things we give to others to keep for us.

—Elbert Hubbard

To keep your secret is wisdom; but to expect others to keep it is folly.

—Samuel Johnson

I have the most perfect confidence in your indiscretion.

—Sydney Smith

Security

Too many people are thinking of security instead of opportunity. They seem more afraid of life than death.

—James F. Byrnes

Each one of us requires the spur of insecurity to force us to do our best.

—Harold W. Dodds

If all that Americans want is security they can go to prison.

—Dwight D. Eisenhower

Distrust and caution are the parents of security.

—Benjamin Franklin

Security is the priceless product of freedom. Only the strong can be secure, and only in freedom can men produce those material resources which can secure them from want at home and against aggression from abroad.

—*B. E. Hutchinson*

Security is mostly a superstition. It does not exist in nature, nor do the children of men as a rule experience it. Avoiding danger is no safer in the long run than outright exposure. Life is either a daring adventure, or nothing.

—*Helen Keller*

Only those means of security are good, are certain, are lasting, that depend on yourself and your own vigor.

—*Niccolo Machiavelli*

Security is a kind of death.

—*Tennessee Williams*

Self-Esteem

It is a poor center of a man's actions, himself.

—*Francis Bacon*

He that falls in love with himself will have no rivals.

—*Benjamin Franklin*

If you are all wrapped up in yourself, you are overdressed.

—Kate Halverson

So many of us define ourselves by what we have, what we wear, what kind of house we live in and what kind of car we drive. If you think of yourself as the woman in the Cartier watch and the Hermes scarf, a house fire will destroy not only your possessions but your self.

—Linda Henley

It is terrible to destroy a person's picture of himself in the interests of truth or some other abstraction.

—Doris Lessing

The most profound relationship we'll ever have is the one with ourselves.

—Shirley MacLaine

Until you make peace with who you are, you'll never be content with what you have.

—Doris Mortman

Nothing is more depressing than the conviction that one is not a hero.

—George Moore

Nobody can make you feel inferior without your consent.

—Eleanor Roosevelt

If we were not all so excessively interested in ourselves, life would be so uninteresting that none of us would be able to endure it.

—*Arthur Schopenhauer*

I have nothing to declare except my genius.

—*Oscar Wilde*

Self-Improvement

There is no use whatever trying to help people who do not help themselves. You cannot push anyone up a ladder unless he be willing to climb himself.

—*Andrew Carnegie*

Keep company with those who may make you better.

—*English proverb*

People seldom improve when they have no other model but themselves to copy after.

—*Oliver Goldsmith*

The improvement of our way of life is more important than the spreading of it. If we make it satisfactory enough, it will spread automatically. If we do not, no strength of arms can permanently oppose it.

—*Charles A. Lindbergh*

I tell you that as long as I can conceive something better than myself I cannot be easy unless I am striving to bring it into existence or clearing the way for it.

—George Bernard Shaw

All of us, who are worth anything, spend our manhood in unlearning the follies, or expiating the mistakes of our youth.

—Percy Bysshe Shelley

Next to being what we ought to be, the most desirable thing is that we should become what we ought to be as fast as possible.

—Herbert Spencer

What you dislike in another take care to correct in yourself.

—Thomas Sprat

Above all, challenge yourself. You may well surprise yourself at what strengths you have, what you can accomplish.

—Cecile M. Springer

Confront the dark parts of yourself, and work to banish them with illumination and forgiveness. Your willingness to wrestle with your demons will cause your angels to sing. Use the pain as fuel, as a reminder of your strength.

—August Wilson

Self-Knowledge

It's not only the most difficult thing to know one's self, but the most inconvenient.

—Josh Billings

No man ever understands quite his own artful dodges to escape from the grim shadow of self-knowledge.

—Joseph Conrad

Know thyself! A maxim as pernicious as it is ugly. Whoever observes himself arrests his own development. A caterpillar who wanted to know itself well would never become a butterfly.

—André Gide

Other men's sins are before our eyes; our own are behind our backs.

—Seneca

We know what we are, but know not what we may be.

—William Shakespeare

I am the only person in the world I should like to know thoroughly.

—Oscar Wilde

Self-Respect

No more duty can be urged upon those who are entering the great theater of life than simple loyalty to their best convictions.

—Edwin Hubbel Chapin

If you want to be respected by others the great thing is to respect yourself. Only by that, only by self-respect will you compel others to respect you.

—*Fyodor Dostoevsky*

It is my ambition and desire to so administer the affairs of the government and remain President that if at the end I have lost every other friend on earth I shall still have one friend remaining and that one shall be down inside me.

—*Abraham Lincoln*

He that respects himself is safe from others; He wears a coat of mail that none can pierce.

—*Henry Wadsworth Longfellow*

Self-respect—the secure feeling that no one, as yet, is suspicious.

—*H. L. Mencken*

It is necessary to the happiness of a man that he be mentally faithful to himself.

—*Thomas Paine*

Learn to value yourself, which means: to fight for your happiness.

—*Ayn Rand*

Have respect for your species. You are a man; do not dishonour mankind.

—*Jean-Jacques Rousseau*

Whatever Talents I possess may suddenly diminish or suddenly increase. I can with ease become an ordinary fool. I may be one now. But it doesn't do to upset one's own vanity.

—Dylan Thomas

Nobody holds a good opinion of a man who has a low opinion of himself.

—Anthony Trollope

When people do not respect us we are sharply offended; yet deep down in his heart no man much respects himself.

—Mark Twain

Do not make yourself low; people will tread on your head.

—Yiddish proverb

Self-Sacrifice
See: Sacrifice

Selling

Murray's Law: Never ask a salesman if his is a good price.

—Arthur Bloch

A bestseller was a book which somehow sold well simply because it was selling well.

—Daniel J. Boorstin

Nothing is as irritating as the fellow that chats pleasantly while he's overcharging you.

—Kin Hubbard

His name was George F. Babbitt. He was forty-six years old now, in April, 1920, and he made nothing in particular, neither butter nor shoes nor poetry, but he was nimble in the calling of selling houses for more than people could afford to pay.

—Sinclair Lewis

For a salesman there is no rock bottom to the life. He don't put a bolt to a nut, he don't tell you the law or give you medicine. He's a man way out there in the blue, riding on a smile and a shoe-shine. And when they start not smiling back—that's an earthquake. And then you get yourself a couple of spots on your hat, and you're finished. A salesman's got to dream, boy. It comes with the territory.

—Arthur Miller

To sell something, tell a woman it's a bargain; tell a man it's deductible.

—Earl Wilson

Sentiment

The barrenest of all mortals is the sentimentalist.

—Thomas Carlyle

Sentimentality—that's what we call the sentiment we don't share.

—Graham Greene

Sentimentality is the only sentiment that rubs you up the wrong way.

—W. Somerset Maugham

A sentimentalist is simply one who desires to have the luxury of an emotion without paying for it.

—Oscar Wilde

Sex

Absence does not make the heart grow fonder, but it sure heats up the blood.

—Elizabeth Ashley

We are minor in everything but our passions.

—Elizabeth Bowen

Modern man speaks of intercourse as "having sex." However, the scriptures never speak this way. In biblical language a man "knows" his wife. It is not an act; it is a relationship.

—Paul Bubna

Cheap sex and precious love; you can't have one if you have the other.

—Jim Conway

The sex drive in the young is a river of fire that must be banked and cooled by a hundred restraints if it is not to consume in chaos both the individual and the group.

—*Will Durant*

Sexuality is what I am and sensuality is how I use it.

—*Sandy Flanigan*

The act of longing for something will always be more intense than the requiting of it.

—*Gail Godwin*

Do not confuse sex, love and intimacy. One does not necessarily imply the other. Experiencing one does not necessarily satisfy our need for the other. While all three ideally come together at certain moments, each of them must be attended to and appreciated. And finally, do not forsake one for the other. You can have them all.

—*Dr. Aaron Hass*

The truth is that wherever a man lies with a woman, there, whether they like it or not, a transcendental relation is set up between them which must be eternally enjoyed or eternally endured.

—*C. S. Lewis*

All really great lovers are articulate, and verbal seduction is the surest road to actual seduction.

—*Marya Mannes*

Sex is good. But don't jump from that to saying that bad sex is better than no sex.

—Eugene O'Sullivan

Never underestimate the power of passion.

—Eve Sawyer

The only sin passion can commit is to be joyless.

—Dorothy Sayers

Sex has become one of the most discussed subjects of modern times. The Victorians pretended it did not exist; the moderns pretend that nothing else exists.

—Bishop Fulton J. Sheen

Sex, like personality, requires intimacy; it calls for veiling. There is no way we can turn it into just another public "fact."

—Bruce Shelley

Sex may be redeemed in our secular age not by denying it and not by indulging it but integrating it into our quest for depth, loyalty, and permanence in interpersonal relationships.

—Edward E. Thornton

Sex: The Gender Gap

In a husband there is only a man; in a married woman there is a man, a father, a mother, and a woman.

—Honoré de Balzac

Every man who is high up likes to feel that he has done it himself; and the wife smiles, and lets it go at that. It's our only joke. Every woman knows that.

—J. M. Barrie

There are more differences within the sexes than between them.

—Guy Compton-Burnett

Most men who rail against women are railing at one woman only.

—Remy de Gourmont

Sometimes I wonder if men and women really suit each other. Perhaps they should live next door and just visit now and then.

—Katharine Hepburn

If Nature had arranged that husbands and wives should have children alternatively, there would never be more than 3 in a family.

—Laurence Housman

Women speak because they wish to speak, whereas a man speaks only when driven to speech by something outside himself—like, for instance, he can't find any clean socks.

—Jean Kerr

The females of all species are most dangerous when they appear to retreat.

—Don Marquis

Man makes love by braggadocio, and woman makes love by listening.

—H. L. Mencken

Women, as they grow older, rely more and more on cosmetics. Men, as they grow older, rely more and more on a sense of humor.

—George Jean Nathan

Women are quite unlike men. Women have higher voices, longer hair, smaller waistlines, daintier feet and prettier hands. They also invariable have the upper hand.

—Stephen Potter

In our civilization, men are afraid that they will not be men enough and women are afraid that they might be considered only women.

—Theodor Reik

A woman may very well form a friendship with a man, but for this to endure, it must be assisted by a little physical antipathy.

—Jean Paul Richter

After an acquaintance of ten minutes many women will exchange confidences that a man would not reveal to a lifelong friend.

—Page Smith

What is most beautiful in virile men is something feminine; what is most beautiful in feminine women is something masculine.

—Susan Sontag

Man is a creature who lives not upon bread alone, but principally by catchwords; and the little rift between the sexes is astonishingly widened by simply teaching one set of catchwords to the girls and another to the boys.

—Robert Louis Stevenson

To women, love is an occupation; to men, a preoccupation.

—Lionel Strachey

Being a sex symbol has to do with an attitude, not looks. Most men think it's looks, most women know otherwise.

—Kathleen Turner

Instead of this absurd division into sexes, they ought to class people as static and dynamic.

—Evelyn Waugh

Men marry because they are tired; women marry because they are curious. Both are disappointed.

—Oscar Wilde

Why are women . . . so much more interesting to men than men are to women

—Virginia Woolf

Men are taught to apologize for their weaknesses, women for their strengths.

—Lois Wyse

Show Business

I beg you to remember that acceptance speeches should be intelligent, witty, and brief. When you leave the stage, your award will be taken from you so that it can be engraved. If you take longer than 30 seconds to accept your award, it will be returned to you eventually, but your name will be misspelled.

—Alexander Cohen

Never tell the box-office man that you can't hear well or he will sell you a seat where you can't see either.

—Kin Hubbard

If you can tune into the fantasy life of an eleven-year-old girl, you can make a fortune in this business.

—George Lucas

Diversify. Learn all you can about acting and singing, as well as dancing. Learn to trust and follow your own instincts. Keep working anywhere you can. And take risks—you don't move forward by staying still.

—Donna McKechnie

My advice to you concerning applause is this: Enjoy it but never quite believe it.

—Robert Montgomery

Here the phony tinsel is stripped away and you can see the real tinsel.

—Mike Romanoff

I've never minded playing a mother. My own mother, who's 87, says: "Keep moving. Then you won't get bitter."

—Eva Marie Saint

Silence

Silence is one of the hardest arguments to refute.

—Josh Billings

If you don't say anything, you won't be called on to repeat it.

—Calvin Coolidge

Silence is the ultimate weapon of power.

—Charles De Gaulle

Blessed is the man who, having nothing to say, abstains from giving wordy evidence of the fact.

—George Eliot

There is no reply so sharp as silent contempt.

—Michel de Montaigne

Silence is the most perfect expression of scorn.

—George Bernard Shaw

Silence may be as variously shaded as speech.

—Edith Wharton

Sin

Confess your sins to the Lord, and you will be forgiven; confess them to men, and you will be laughed at.

—*Josh Billings*

That which we call sin in others, is experiment for us.

—*Ralph Waldo Emerson*

Sin is not harmful because it is forbidden, but it is forbidden because it is hurtful.

—*Benjamin Franklin*

Sin writes histories, goodness is silent.

—*Goethe*

Men are not punished for their sins, but by them.

—*Elbert Hubbard*

All human sin seems so much worse in its consequences than in its intentions.

—*Reinhold Niebuhr*

Sin means that our reason is warped by our pride.

—*Robert Raines*

Whatever weakens your reason, impairs the tenderness of conscience, obscures your sense of God, takes the relish off spiritual things, this is sin to you.

—*Susanna Wesley*

Skepticism

Skepticism is the first step on the road to philosophy.

—Denis Diderot

I respect faith, but doubt is what gets you an education.

—Wilson Mizner

The path of sound credence is through the thick forest of skepticism.

—George Jean Nathan

Great intellects are skeptical.

—Friedrich Nietzsche

Skepticism, riddling the faith of yesterday, prepared the way for the faith of tomorrow.

—Romain Rolland

Sleep

Living is a disease from which sleep gives us relief eight hours a day.

—Chamfort

Sleep lingers all our lifetime about our eyes, as night hovers all day in the boughs of the fir-tree.

—Ralph Waldo Emerson

Fatigue is the best pillow.

—Benjamin Franklin

Sleep is when all the unsorted stuff comes flying out as from a dustbin upset in a high wind.

—William Golding

We are not hypocrites in our sleep.

—William Hazlitt

Cultivate the habit of early rising. It is unwise to keep the head long on a level with the feet.

—Henry David Thoreau

Smoking

The best way to stop smoking is to carry wet matches.

—Anonymous

I know a man who gave up smoking, drink, sex, and rich food. He was healthy right up to the time he killed himself.

—Johnny Carson

I must point out that my rule of life prescribed as an absolute sacred rite smoking cigars and also the drinking of alcohol before, after, and if need be during all meals and in the intervals between them.

—Winston Churchill

Smokers, male and female, inject and excuse idleness in their lives every time they light a cigarette.

—Colette

Tobacco is the tomb of love.

—Benjamin Disraeli

The believing we do something when we do nothing is the first illusion of tobacco.

—Ralph Waldo Emerson

Tobacco surely was designed
To poison, and destroy mankind.

—Philip Freneau

But when I don't smoke I scarcely feel as if I'm living. I don't feel as if I'm living unless I'm killing myself.

—Russell Hoban

A custom loathsome to the eye, hateful to the nose, harmful to the brain, dangerous to the lungs, and in the black, stinking fumes thereof, nearest resembling the horrible Stygian smoke of the pit that is bottomless.

—King James I

Smoking is a shocking thing, blowing smoke out of our mouths into other people's mouths, eyes, and noses, and having the same thing done to us.

—Samuel Johnson

The tobacco business is a conspiracy against womanhood and manhood. It owes its origin to that scoundrel Sir Walter Raleigh, who was likewise the founder of American slavery.

—John Harvey Kellogg

I tried to stop smoking cigarettes by telling myself I just didn't want to smoke, but I didn't believe myself.

—Barbara Kelly

Smoking is one of the leading causes of statistics.

—Fletcher Knebel

Smoking is, as far as I'm concerned, the entire point of being an adult.

—Fran Lebowitz

It is more profitable for your congressman to support the tobacco industry than your life.

—Jackie Mason

There's nothing quite like tobacco; it's the passion of decent folk, and whoever lives without tobacco doesn't deserve to live.

—Molière

This vice brings in one hundred million francs in taxes every year. I will certainly forbid it at once—as soon as you can name a virtue that brings in as much revenue.

—Napoleon III

Much smoking kills live men and cures dead swine.

—George D. Prentice

I have every sympathy with the American who was so horrified by what he had read of the effects of smoking that he gave up reading.

—Henry G. Strauss

I kissed my first woman and smoked my first cigarette on the same day; I have never had time for tobacco since.

—Arturo Toscanini

To cease smoking is the easiest thing I ever did; I ought to know because I've done it a thousand times.

—Mark Twain

There are people who strictly deprive themselves of each and every eatable, drinkable and smokable which has in any way acquired a shady reputation. They pay this price for health.

—Mark Twain

Pipe smokers spend so much time cleaning, filling, and fooling with their pipes, they don't have time to get into mischief.

—Bill Vaughan

A cigarette is the perfect type of a perfect pleasure. It is exquisite, and it leaves one unsatisfied. What more can one want?

—Oscar Wilde

Society

Society is like a lawn where every roughness is smoothed, every bramble eradicated, and where the eye is delighted by the smiling verdure of a velvet surface.

—Washington Irving

Giving parties is a trivial avocation, but it pays the dues for my union card in humanity.

—Elsa Maxwell

Society attacks early when the individual is helpless.

—B. F. Skinner

Society is a madhouse whose wardens are the officials and police.

—August Strindberg

To get into the best society nowadays, one has either to feed people, amuse people, or shock people.

—Oscar Wilde

Society can only exist on the basis that there is some amount of polished lying and that no one says exactly what he thinks.

—Lin Yutang

Soldiers

Every French soldier carries in his cartridge-pouch the baton of a marshal of France.

—Napoleon Bonaparte

The mounted knight is irresistible; he would bore his way through the walls of Babylon.

—Anna Comnena

The patriot volunteer, fighting for country and his rights, makes the most reliable soldier on earth.

—Stonewall Jackson

Honor to the Soldier, and Sailor everywhere, who bravely bears his country's cause, Honor also to the citizen who cares for his brother in the field, and serves, as he best can, the same cause—honor to him, only less than to him, who braves, for the common good, the storm of heaven and the storms of battle.

—Abraham Lincoln

The soldier, above all other men, is required to perform the highest act of religious offering—sacrifice. In battle and in the face of danger and death he discloses those divine attributes which his Maker gave when he created man in his own image. No physical courage and no brute instincts can take the place of the divine annunciation and spiritual gift which will alone sustain him.

—Douglas MacArthur

They're changing guard at Buckingham
  Palace—
Christopher Robin went down with Alice.
Alice is marrying one of the guard.
"A soldier's life is terrible hard,"
Says Alice.

—A. A. Milne

An atheist could not be as great a military leader as one who is not an atheist.

—Thomas H. Moorer

Then was seen with what a strength and majesty the British soldier fights.

—William Napier

It is foolish and wrong to mourn the men who died. Rather we should thank God that such men lived.

—George S. Patton

The soldier's body becomes a stock of accessories that are not his property.

—Antoine de Saint-Exupéry

In the great hour of destiny they stand,
Each with his feuds, his jealousies, his sorrows.
Soldiers are sworn to action; they must win
Some flaming, fatal climax with their lives.
Soldiers are dreamers, when the guns begin
They think of firelit homes, clean beds,
  and wives.

—Siegfried Sassoon

Solitude

You can always tell an old soldier by the inside of his holsters and cartridge box. The young ones carry pistols and cartridges; the old ones, grub.

—*George Bernard Shaw*

Solitude

Whoever is delighted in solitude is either a wild beast or a god.

—*Francis Bacon*

Solitude: A good place to visit, but a poor place to stay.

—*Josh Billings*

The right to be alone—the most comprehensive of rights, and the right most valued by civilized man.

—*Louis D. Brandeis*

I live in that solitude which is painful in youth, but delicious in the years of maturity.

—*Albert Einstein*

I never found the companion that was so companionable as solitude.

—*Henry David Thoreau*

The happiest of all lives is a busy solitude.

—*Voltaire*

Sorrow

See also: Grief

Sorrow makes men sincere.

—Henry Ward Beecher

This is my last message to you: in sorrow seek happiness.

—Feodor Dostoevsky

Earth hath no sorrow that heaven cannot heal.

—Thomas Moore

Sorrows are like thunderclouds. Far off they look black, but directly over us merely gray.

—Jean Paul Richter

There can be no rainbow without a cloud and a storm.

—J. H. Vincent

Space

The question is not so much whether there is life on Mars as whether it will continue to be possible to live on Earth.

—Anonymous

Walking in space, man has never looked more puny or more significant.

—Alexander Chase

Today we can no more predict what use mankind may make of the Moon than could Columbus have imagined the future of the continent he had discovered.

—*Arthur C. Clarke*

I suppose the one quality in astronauts more powerful than any other is curiosity. They have to get some place nobody's ever been before.

—*John Glenn*

Space isn't remote at all. It's only an hour's drive away if your car could go straight upwards.

—*Sir Fred Hoyle*

Speech

See also: Arts: Writing; Books and Reading; Words

Speech is power: speech is to persuade, to convert, to compel.

—*Ralph Waldo Emerson*

Half the world is composed of people who have something to say and can't, and the other half who have nothing to say and keep on saying it.

—*Robert Frost*

Many a man's tongue broke his nose.

—*Seamus MacManus*

All speech, written or spoke, is a dead language, until it finds a willing and prepared hearer.

—*Robert Louis Stevenson*

It usually takes more than three weeks to prepare a good impromptu speech.

—Mark Twain

Spirituality

Great men are they who see that the spiritual is stronger than any material force.

—Ralph Waldo Emerson

We deny the existence of spirit and then are helpless before it's raw power. We talk much about it, then refuse to live as though it really matters.

—Arnold Rampersad

One truth stands firm. All that happens in world history rests on something spiritual. If the spiritual is strong, it creates world history. If it is weak, it suffers world history.

—Albert Schweitzer

Pressed, I would define spirituality as the shadow of light humanity casts as it moves through the darkness of everything that can't be explained.

—John Updike

Sports

If you want to meet new people, pick up the wrong golf ball.

—Anonymous

If the people don't want to come out to the park, nobody's gonna stop them.

—Yogi Berra

You've got to take the initiative and play your game. In a decisive set, confidence is the difference.

—Chris Evert

Nolan Ryan is pitching a lot better now that he has his curve ball straightened out.

—Joe Garagiola

I don't think we can win every game. Just the next one.

—Lou Holtz

Winning is not everything. It's the only thing.

—Vince Lombardi

Serious sport has nothing to do with fair play. It is bound up with hatred, jealousy, boastfulness, disregard of all rules and sadistic pleasure in witnessing violence: in other words it is war minus the shooting.

—George Orwell

I'm no different from anybody else with two arms, two legs, and forty-two hundred hits.

—Pete Rose

I always turn to the sports pages first, which record people's accomplishments. The front page has nothing but man's failures.

—Chief Justice Earl Warren

Strength

The strength of a man consists in finding out the way God is going, and going that way.

—Henry Ward Beecher

There may come a time when the lion and the lamb will lie down together, but I am still betting on the lion.

—Josh Billings

Calmness and irony are the only weapons worthy of the strong.

—Emile Gaboriau

There is only one right in the world and that right is one's own strength.

—Adolf Hitler

Strength without gentleness is tyranny.

—Joanne D. Holland

Sorrow and silence are strong, and patient endurance is godlike.

—Henry Wadsworth Longfellow

We have enough strength to endure the misfortunes of others.

—François de la Rochefoucauld

My strength is as the strength of ten,
Because my heart is pure.

—Lord Tennyson

Stress

It is from weakness that people reach for dictators and concentrated government power. Only the strong can be free. And only the productive can be strong.

—Wendell Willkie

Stress

The rule is, jam tomorrow and jam yesterday—but never jam today.

—Lewis Carroll

Learn not to sweat the small stuff.

—Dr. Kenneth Greenspan

All the irritations of daily life subject your mind and nerves and then your muscles, to repeated tension. You can work out most of this tension with your exercise program, but if you are smart, you will try to avoid most of the tension to begin with.

—Dr. Leon Root

Style

To me style is just the outside of content, and content the inside of style, like the outside and the inside of the human body—both go together, they can't be separated.

—Jean-Luc Goddard

Style is the hallmark of a temperament stamped upon the material at hand.

—Andre Maurois

Fashions fade, style is eternal.

—Yves St. Laurent

Properly understood style is not a seductive decoration added to a functional structure; it is of the essence of a work of art.

—Evelyn Waugh

Success

See also: Ambition; Accomplishment/Achievement

Be commonplace and creeping and you will be a success.

—Pierre de Beaumarchais

The toughest thing about success is that you've got to keep on being a success. Talent is only a starting point in this business.

—Irving Berlin

Success is the one unpardonable sin against one's fellows.

—Ambrose Bierce

Try not to become a man of success but rather try to become a man of value.

—Albert Einstein

Success has ruined many a man.

—Benjamin Franklin

It's not that I'm not grateful for all this attention. It's just that fame and fortune ought to add up to more than fame and fortune.

—Robert Fulghum

Nothing succeeds like the appearance of success.

—Christopher Lasch

Success or failure lies in conformity to the times.

—Niccolo Machiavelli

All you need in this life is ignorance and confidence, and then Success is sure.

—Mark Twain

It is not enough to succeed; others must fail.

—Gore Vidal

Suffering

See also: Grief; Sorrow

By suffering comes wisdom.

—Aeschylus

Man cannot remake himself without suffering. For he is both the marble and the sculptor.

—Alexis Carrel

Man, the bravest of the animals and the one most inured to suffering.

—Friedrich Nietzsche

It is not true that suffering ennobles the character; happiness does that sometimes, but suffering, for the most part, makes men petty and vindictive.

—*W. Somerset Maugham*

Grief can take care of itself, but to get the full value of joy you must have somebody to divide it with.

—*Mark Twain*

Misfortunes one can endure—they come from outside, they are accidents. But to suffer for one's own faults—ah, there is the sting of life.

—*Oscar Wilde*

Suicide

To run away from trouble is a form of cowardice and, while it is true that the suicide braves death, he does it not for some noble object but to escape some ill.

—*Aristotle*

There are many who dare not kill themselves for fear of what the neighbors will say.

—*Cyril Connolly*

Suicide is belated acquiescence in the opinion of one's wife's relatives.

—*H. L. Mencken*

Survival

The thought of suicide is a great consolation: with the help of it one has got through many a bad night.

—*Friedrich Nietzsche*

I don't think suicide is so terrible. Some rainy winter Sundays when there's a little boredom, you should always carry a gun. Not to shoot yourself, but to know exactly that you're always making a choice.

—*Lina Wertmuller*

Survival

I haven't asked you to make me young again. All I want is to go on getting older.

—*Konrad Adenauer*

Before undergoing a surgical operation arrange your temporal affairs. You may live.

—*Ambrose Bierce*

It is not important to come out on top; what matters is to come out alive.

—*Bertolt Brecht*

Nothing in life is so exhilarating as to be shot at without result.

—*Winston Churchill*

If you live among wolves you have to act like a wolf.

—*Nikita Khrushchev*

To survive it is often necessary to fight, and to fight you have to dirty yourself.

—George Orwell

The growth of a large business is merely a survival of the fittest.

—John D. Rockefeller

When you get to the end of your rope, tie a knot and hang on.

—Franklin D. Roosevelt

The thing-in-itself, the will-to-live, exists whole and undivided in every being, even in the tiniest; it is present as completely as in all that ever were, are, and will be, taken together.

—Arthur Schopenhauer

To win your battle in this society, you've got to have your cave. Then food. Then some kind of mate. After that, everything's a luxury.

—Rod Steiger

Put fear out of your heart. This nation will survive, this state will prosper, the orderly business of life will go forward if only men can speak in whatever way given them to utter what their hearts hold—by voice, by posted card, by letters or by press. Reason never has failed them. Only force and oppression have made the wrecks in the world.

—William Allen White

One can survive anything these days except death.

—Oscar Wilde

Sympathy

The truest help we can render an afflicted man is not to take his burden from him, but to call out his best strength that he may be able to bear the burden.

—Phillips Brooks

We should spread joy, but cut down sadness as much as we can. He who asks for pity without reason is a man not to be pitied when there is reason. By continually putting on a pitiful act, we become pitiable to no one.

—Michel de Montaigne

Being unwanted, unloved, uncared for, forgotten by everybody, I think that is a much greater hunger, a much greater poverty than the person who has nothing to eat. We must find each other.

—Mother Teresa

Do not believe that he who seeks to comfort you lives untroubled among the simple and quiet words that sometimes do you good. His life has much difficulty and sadness and remains far behind yours. Were it otherwise he would never have been able to find those words.

—Rainer Maria Rilke

When you see a man in distress, recognize him as a fellow man.

—Seneca

Sympathy is a thing to be encouraged apart from humane consideration, because it supplies us with the materials for wisdom.

—Robert Louis Stevenson

T

Tact

Tact consists of knowing how far we may go too far.

—Jean Cocteau

Without tact you can learn nothing.

—Benjamin Disraeli

Tact: to lie about others as you would have them lie about you.

—Oliver Herford

Be kind and considerate to others, depending somewhat upon who they are.

—Don Herold

Taste

It's bad manners to begin courting a widow before she gets home from the funeral.

—Seamus MacManus

Taste

Bad taste is a species of bad morals.

—Christian Nestell Bovee

Taste is the feminine of genius.

—Edward Fitzgerald

No one ever went broke underestimating the taste of the American public.

—H. L. Mencken

Taste is the enemy of creativeness.

—Pablo Picasso

Taste is the only morality . . . Tell me what you like, and I'll tell you what you are.

—John Ruskin

A man of great common sense and good taste—thereby a man without originality or moral courage.

—George Bernard Shaw

Good taste is the excuse I've always given for leading such a bad life.

—Oscar Wilde

Tax

The art of taxation consists in so plucking the goose as to obtain the largest amount of feathers with the least possible amount of hissing.

—J. B. Colbert

For every benefit you receive a tax is levied.

—Ralph Waldo Emerson

I'm proud to pay taxes in the United States; the only thing is, I could be just as proud for half the money.

—Arthur Godfrey

Never before have so many been taken for so much and left with so little.

—Van Panopoulos

Taxes cause crime. When the tax rate reaches 25 percent, there is an increase in lawlessness. America's tax system is inspired by Karl Marx.

—Ronald Reagan

The income tax has made more liars out of the American people than gold has.

—Will Rogers

A government which robs Peter to pay Paul can always depend on the support of Paul.

—George Bernard Shaw

What is the difference between a taxidermist and a tax collector? The taxidermist takes only your skin.

—Mark Twain

Teaching

See also: Education; Knowledge; Learning

A teacher affects eternity.

—Henry B. Adams

It is the supreme art of the teacher to awaken joy in creative expression and knowledge.

—Albert Einstein

Knowledge exists to be imparted.

—Ralph Waldo Emerson

You cannot teach a man anything; you can only help him find it within himself.

—Galileo

The teacher is one who makes two ideas grow where only one grew before.

—Elbert Hubbard

He who can, does. He who cannot, teaches.

—George Bernard Shaw

To be good is noble, but to teach others how to be good is nobler—and less trouble.

—Mark Twain

Everybody who is incapable of learning has taken to teaching.

—Oscar Wilde

Technology

See also: Science; Space; Television

Any sufficiently advanced technology is indistinguishable from magic.

—Arthur C. Clarke

As nuclear and other technological achievements continue to mount, the normal life span will continue to climb. The hourly productivity of the worker will increase.

—Dwight D. Eisenhower

The economic and technological triumphs of the past few years have not solved as many problems as we thought they would, and, in fact, have brought us new problems we did not foresee.

—Henry Ford II

One machine can do the work of fifty ordinary men. No machine can do the work of one extraordinary man.

—Elbert Hubbard

Television

Television is a device that permits people who haven't anything to do watch people who can't do anything.

—Fred Allen

Television is democracy at its ugliest.

—Paddy Chayevsky

You have debased [my] child. You have made him a laughing stock of intelligence . . . a stench in the nostrils of the ionosphere.

—Lee DeForest

My father hated radio and could not wait for television to be invented so he could hate that too.

—Peter De Vries

Television is an invention that permits you to be entertained in your living room by people you wouldn't have in your home.

—David Frost

Television—a medium. So called because it is neither rare nor well done.

—Ernie Kovacs

Television is a corporate vulgarity.

—John Leonard

I must say I find television very educational. The minute somebody turns it on, I go to the library and read a good book.

—Groucho Marx

Television is the source of our most powerful collective memories.

—Michael Winshop

Television is chewing gum for the eyes.

—Frank Lloyd Wright

Temptation

See also: Passion

Lead me not into temptation; I can find the way myself.

—Rita Mae Brown

Better shun the bait than struggle in the snare.

—John Dryden

Temptation is an irresistible force at work on a movable body.

—H. L. Mencken

There are several good protections against temptation, but the surest is cowardice.

—Mark Twain

Few men have virtue to withstand the highest bidder.

—George Washington

Thanksgiving

Stand up, on this Thanksgiving Day, stand upon your feet. Believe in man. Soberly, and with clear eyes, believe in your own time and place.

—Phillips Brooks

A thankful heart is not only the greatest virtue, but the parent of all other virtues.

—Cicero

Not what we say about our blessings but how we use them is the true message of our thanksgiving.

—W. T. Purkiser

The pilgrims made seven times more graves than huts. No Americans have been more impoverished than those—who, nevertheless, set aside a day of thanksgiving.

—H. W. Westermeyer

Theology

See also: Christianity; God; Religion

Theology is a science of mind applied to God.

—Henry Ward Beecher

It is the task of theology not to get drunk with foreign ideas and beat up on God's children, but to feed and strengthen them.

—Klaus Bockmuhl

I would rather feel contrition than know how to define it.

—Thomas à Kempis

Theology is the effort to explain the unknowable in terms of the not worth knowing.

—H. L. Mencken

Division has done more to hide Christ from the view of all men than all the infidelity that has ever been spoken.

—George MacDonald

Theory

It is a capital mistake to theorize before one has data.

—Sir Arthur Conan Doyle

A theory can be proved by experiment; but no path leads from experiment to the birth of a theory.

—Albert Einstein

No theory is good except on condition that one uses it to go beyond.

—André Gide

A young boy is a theory, an old man is a fact.

—Ed Howe

In scientific work, those who refuse to go beyond fact rarely get as far as fact.

—Thomas Huxley

Thought

See also: Action; Ideas; Language

Great thought reduced to practice become great acts.

—William Hazlitt

Thought takes man out of servitude, into freedom.

—Henry Wadsworth Longfellow

I've know countless people who were reservoirs of learning yet never had a thought.

—Wilson Mizner

It is difficult, if not impossible, for most people to think otherwise than in the fashion of their own period.

—George Bernard Shaw

Sixty minutes of thinking of any kind is bound to lead to confusion and unhappiness.

—James Thurber

Men use thought only to justify their injustices, and speech only to disguise their thoughts.

—Voltaire

Time

See also: Rest; Waste

Lost time is never found again.

—John H. Aughey

Time was invented by God to give ideas a chance.

—Nicholas Murray Butler

Does't thou love life? Then do not squander time, for that is the stuff life is made of.

—Benjamin Franklin

Time and tide wait for no man, but time always stands still for a woman of 30.

—Robert Frost

Consider, Sir, how insignificant this will appear a twelve-month hence.

—Samuel Johnson

We must use time as a tool, not as a couch.

—John F. Kennedy

Time is a storm in which we are all lost.

—William Carlos Williams

Tolerance

See also: Prejudice; Rights

The responsibility of tolerance lies in those who have the wider vision.

—George Eliot

Tolerance comes with age. I see no fault committed that I myself could not have committed at some time or other.

—Goethe

Toleration . . . is the greatest gift of the mind; it requires the same effort of the brain that it takes to balance oneself on a bicycle.

—Helen Keller

Broadminded is just another way of saying a fellow's too lazy to form an opinion.

—Will Rogers

To understand everything makes one very indulgent.

—Madame de Staël

Tradition

See also: Custom

Tradition means giving votes to the most obscure of all classes—our ancestors. It is the democracy of the dead. Tradition refuses to submit to the small and arrogant oligarchy of those who merely happen to be walking around.

—*G. K. Chesterton*

A precedent embalms a principle.

—*Benjamin Disraeli*

Traditionalists are pessimists about the future and optimists about the past.

—*Lewis Mumford*

The longer I live the more keenly I feel that what ever was good enough for our fathers is not good enough for us.

—*Oscar Wilde*

Tragedy

See also: Arts: Acting and Drama

What the American public wants in the theater is a tragedy with a happy ending.

—*William D. Howells*

Where the theater is concerned, one must have a dream and the Greek dream in tragedy is the noblest ever.

—*Eugene O'Neill*

There are two tragedies in life: one is to lose your heart's desire, the other is to gain it.

—*George Bernard Shaw*

We begin to live when we have conceived life as a tragedy.

—*William Butler Yeats*

Travel

The most common of all antagonisms arises from a man's taking a seat beside you on the train, a seat to which he is completely entitled.

—*Robert Benchley*

When one realizes that his life is worthless he either commits suicide or travels.

—*Edward Dahlberg*

People travel for the same reason as they collect works of art: because the best people do it.

—*Aldous Huxley*

I always say that a girl never really looks as well as she does on board a steamship, or even a yacht.

—*Anita Loos*

To travel hopefully is a better thing than to arrive.

—*Robert Louis Stevenson*

Extensive traveling induces a feeling of encapsulation, and travel, so broadening at first, contracts the mind.

—Paul Theroux

Treason

See also: Patriotism; Rebellion

Treason is loved of many, but the traitor hated of all.

—Robert Greene

Treason is like diamonds; there is nothing to be made by the small trader.

—Douglas Jerrold

Combinations of wickedness would overwhelm the world did not those who have long practiced perfidy grow faithless to each other.

—Samuel Johnson

Write on my gravestone: "Infidel, Traitor."—infidel to every church that compromises with wrong; traitor to every government that oppresses the people.

—Wendell Phillips

Trouble

See also: Anxiety

Now one of the great reasons why so many husbands and wives make shipwrecks of their lives together is because a man is always seeking for happiness, while a woman is on a perpetual still hunt for trouble.

—Dorothy Dix

Trouble is only opportunity in work clothes.

—Henry J. Kaiser

The only incurable troubles of the rich are the troubles that money can't cure, which is a kind of trouble that is even more troublesome if you are poor.

—Ogden Nash

Truth

See also: Diplomacy; Prejudice

There's an element of truth in every idea that lasts long enough to be called corny.

—Irving Berlin

Truth gets well if she is run over by a locomotive, while error dies of lockjaw if she scratches her finger.

—William Cullen Bryant

Men occasionally stumble over the truth, but most of them pick themselves up and hurry off as if nothing had happened.

—Winston Churchill

Truth is shorter than fiction.

—Irving Cohen

That's not a lie, it's a terminological inexactitude.

—Alexander Haig

The truth of a proposition has nothing to do with its credibility. And vice versa.

—Robert Heinlein

It is hard to believe that a man is telling the truth when you know that you would lie if you were in his place.

—H. L. Mencken

Never tell the truth to people who are not worthy of it.

—Mark Twain

The pure and simple truth is rarely pure and never simple.

—Oscar Wilde

Tyranny

See also: Communism; Conscience; Rebellion

It is far easier to act under conditions of tyranny than to think.

—Hannah Arendt

Tyranny and anarchy are never far asunder.

—*Jeremy Bentham*

In the groves of their academy, at the end of every vista, you see nothing but the gallows.

—*Edmund Burke*

Every tyrant who has lived has believed in freedom—for himself.

—*Elbert Hubbard*

There are few minds to which tyranny is not delightful.

—*Samuel Johnson*

Tyrants have always some slight shade of virtue; they support the laws before destroying them.

—*Voltaire*

U

Ugliness

See also: Beauty

There is a sort of charm in ugliness, if the person has some redeeming qualities and is only ugly enough.

—*Josh Billings*

Understanding

It was not until I had attended a few postmortems that I realized that even the ugliest human exteriors may contain the most beautiful viscera, and was able to console myself for the facial drabness of my neighbors in omnibuses by dissecting them in my imagination.

—*J. B. S. Haldane*

Understanding

What you cannot understand, you cannot possess.

—*Goethe*

He who does not understand your silence will probably not understand your words.

—*Elbert Hubbard*

If one does not understand a person, one tends to regard him as a fool.

—*Carl Jung*

Shallow understanding from people of good will is more frustrating than absolute misunderstanding from people of ill-will.

—*Martin Luther King, Jr.*

If you are sure you understand everything that is going on, you are hopelessly confused.

—*Walter F. Mondale*

It is difficult to get a man to understand something when his salary depends upon his not understanding it.

—*Upton Sinclair*

Unity

See also: Loyalty; Strength

Men's hearts ought not to be set against one another, but set with one another, and all against evil only.

—*Thomas Carlyle*

We must hang together or assuredly we shall hang separately.

—*Benjamin Franklin*

Unity to be real must stand the severest strain without breaking.

—*Mahatma Gandhi*

Universe

In this unbelievable universe in which we live there are no absolutes. Even parallel lines, reaching into infinity, meet somewhere yonder.

—*Pearl S. Buck*

The Universe is but one vast symbol of God.

—*Thomas Carlyle*

Know that you are a part of the whole scheme of things—a part of the universe.

—*Buckminster Fuller*

The universe begins to look more like a great thought than a great machine.

—James Jeans

My theology, briefly, is that the universe was dictated, but not signed.

—Christopher Morley

Great is this organism of mud and fire, terrible this vast, painful, glorious experiment.

—George Santayana

V

Vacation

See also: Rest

The rainy days a man saves for usually seem to arrive during his vacation.

—Anonymous

No man needs a vacation so much as the man who has just had one.

—Elbert Hubbard

If some people didn't tell you, you'd never know they'd been away on a vacation.

—Kin Hubbard

Values

See also: Civilization; Success

Teach us that wealth is not elegance, that profusion is not magnificence, that splendor is not beauty.

—Benjamin Disraeli

All that is valuable in human society depends upon the opportunity for development accorded the individual.

—Albert Einstein

It is not our affluence, or our plumbing, or our clogged freeways that grip the imagination of others. Rather, it is the values upon which our system is built. These values imply our adherence not only to liberty and individual freedom, but also to international peace, law and order, and constructive social purpose. When we depart from these values, we do so at our peril.

—J. William Fulbright

Religion is the sole technique for the validating of values.

—Allen Tate

Vanity

See also: Fame

Vain-glorious men are the scorn of the wise, the admiration of fools, the idols of paradise, and the slaves of their own vaunts.

—Francis Bacon

The only cure for vanity is laughter, and the only fault that's laughable is vanity.

—Henri Bergson

We are so vain that we even care for the opinion of those we don't care for.

—Marie von Ebner-Eschenbach

The best way to turn a woman's head is to tell her she has a beautiful profile.

—-Sacha Guitry

The time he can spare from the adornment of his person he devotes to the neglect of his duties.

—Samuel Johnson

Vengeance

See also: Anger; Hate

Revenge is a kind of wild justice, which the more a man's nature runs to, the more ought law to weed it out.

—Francis Bacon

The devil himself has not yet created a suitable vengeance for the blood of a slain infant.

—Menachem Begin

Nothing is more costly, nothing is more sterile, than vengeance.

—Sir Winston Churchill

The best manner of avenging ourselves is by not resembling him who has injured us.

—Jane Porter

The best revenge is to live long enough to be a problem to your children.

—*Unknown*

Vice

See also: Crime; Evil; Sin

Vice is a creature of such hideous mien that the more you see it the better you like it.

—*Finley Peter Dunne*

Many a man's vices have at first been nothing worse than good qualities run wild.

—*Augustus and Julius Hare*

One big vice in a man is apt to keep out a great many smaller ones.

—*Bret Harte*

A little of what you fancy does you good.

—*Marie Lloyd*

It seems impossible to root out of an Englishman's mind the notion that vice is delightful, and that abstention from it is privation.

—*George Bernard Shaw*

He hasn't a single redeeming vice.

—*Oscar Wilde*

Victory

The most important thing in the Olympic games is not winning but taking part . . . The essential thing in life is not conquering but fighting well.

—Pierre de Coubertin

We should wage war not to win war, but to win peace.

—Paul Hoffman

Victory and defeat are each of the same price.

—Thomas Jefferson

Whether in chains or in laurels, liberty knows nothing but victories.

—Douglas MacArthur

Vietnam

As Ed Murrow once said about Vietnam, anyone who isn't confused doesn't really understand the situation.

—Walter Bryan

Would this sort of war or savage bombing which has taken place in Vietnam have been tolerated for so long had the people been European?

—Indira Gandhi

Above all, Vietnam was a war that asked everything of a few and nothing of most in America.

—Myra McPherson

North Vietnam cannot defeat or humiliate the United States. Only Americans can do that.

—Richard Nixon

To win in Vietnam, we will have to exterminate a nation.

—Benjamin Spock

Violence

See also: Anger

I write about violence as naturally as Jane Austen wrote about manners. Violence shapes and obsesses our society, and if we do not stop being violent we have no future.

—Edward Bond

All violence, all that is dreary and repels, is not power, but the absence of power.

—Ralph Waldo Emerson

Nothing good ever comes of violence.

—Martin Luther

In violence we forget who we are.

—Mary McCarthy

Virtue

If you can be well without health, you may be happy without virtue.

—Edmund Burke

There are few good women who do not tire of their role.

—François, Duc de La Rochefoucauld

If he does really think there is no distinction between virtue and vice, why, sir, when he leaves our houses let us count our spoons.

—Samuel Johnson

Woman's virtue is man's greatest invention.

—Cornelia Otis Skinner

What men call social virtues, good fellowship, is commonly but the virtue of pigs in a litter, which lie close together to keep each other warm.

—Henry David Thoreau

Virtue has never been as respectable as money.

—Mark Twain

Virtue has its own reward, but no sale at the box office.

—Mae West

It is always one's virtues and not one's vices that precipitate one into disaster.

—Rebecca West

Vision

The farther back you can look, the farther forward you are likely to see.

—Winston Churchill

It seems to me we can never give up longing and wishing while we are alive. There are certain things we feel to be beautiful and good, and we must hunger for them.

—George Eliot

I just want to do God's will. And he's allowed me to go up to the mountain. And I've looked over, and I've seen the Promised Land.

—Martin Luther King, Jr.

The visionary lies to himself; the liar only to others.

—Friedrich Nietzsche

You see things; and say "Why?" But I dream things that never were and I say "Why not?"

—George Bernard Shaw

Vote

See also: America and Americans; Democracy; Patriotism

Vote for the man who promises least—he'll be the least disappointing.

—Bernard Baruch

I never vote for anyone. I always vote against.

—W. C. Fields

Giving every man a vote has no more made men wise and free than Christianity has made them good.

—H. L. Mencken

When a fellow tells me he's bipartisan, I know he's going to vote against me.

—Harry S Truman

W

Wage

See also: Capitalism; Labor

Low wages are not cheap wages.

—Louis D. Brandeis

The high wage begins down in the shop. If it is not created there it cannot get into pay envelopes. There will never be a system invented which will do away with the necessity for work.

—Henry Ford

No business which depends for existence on paying less than living wages to its workers has any right to continue in this country.

—Franklin D. Roosevelt

Men who do things without being told draw the most wages.

—Edwin H. Stuart

War

See also: Diplomacy; Peace

Human war has been the most successful of our cultural traditions.

—Robert Ardrey

Soldiers usually win the battles and generals get the credit for them.

—Napoleon Bonaparte

War is like love; it always finds a way.

—Bertolt Brecht

No one can guarantee success in war, but only deserve it.

—Winston Churchill

That brother should not war with brother,
And worry and devour each other.

—William Cowper

War is the trade of kings.

—John Dryden

As long as there are sovereign nations possessing great power, war is inevitable.

—Albert Einstein

There never was a good war or a bad peace.

—Benjamin Franklin

I have never advocated war except as a means for peace.

—Ulysses S. Grant

I'd like to see the government get out of war altogether and leave the whole feud to private industry.

—Joseph Heller

War is, at first, the hope that we will be better off; next, the expectation that the other fellow will be worse off; then, the satisfaction that he isn't any better off; and, finally, the surprise at everyone's being worse off.

—Karl Kraus

It is well that war is so terrible—we shouldn't grow too fond of it.

—Robert E. Lee

The belief in the possibility of a short decisive war appears to be one of the most ancient and dangerous of human illusions.

—Robert Lynd

War hath no fury like a noncombatant.

—C. E. Montague

Diplomats are just as essential in starting a war as soldiers are in finishing it.

—Will Rogers

As long as war is regarded as wicked, it will always have its fascination. When it is looked upon as vulgar, it will cease to be popular.

—Oscar Wilde

Waste

See also: Loss; Time

I wish I could stand on a busy street corner, hat in hand, and beg people to throw me all their wasted hours.

—Bernard Berenson

A man who dares to waste one hour of life has not discovered the value of life.

—Charles Darwin

Waste neither time nor money, but make the best use of both. Without industry and frugality, nothing will do, and with them everything.

—Benjamin Franklin

Weakness

See also: Cowardice; Pride

Better make a weak man your enemy than your friend.

—Josh Billings

A weak mind is like a microscope, which magnifies trifling things but cannot receive great ones.

—Lord Chesterfield

We must have a weak spot or two in our character before we can love it much.

—Oliver Wendell Holmes

You cannot run away from weakness; you must some time fight it out or perish; and if that be so, why not now, and where you stand?

—Robert Louis Stevenson

Wealth

See also: Capitalism; Money

It is the interest of the commercial world that wealth should be found everywhere.

—Edmund Burke

Surplus wealth is a sacred trust which its possessor is bound to administer in his lifetime for the good of the community.

—Andrew Carnegie

The gratification of wealth is not found in mere possession or in lavish expenditure, but in its wise application.

—Miguel de Cervantes

Wealth is not without its advantages and the case to the contrary, although it has often been made, has never proved widely persuasive.

—John Kenneth Galbraith

If you can actually count your money then you are not really a rich man.

—J. Paul Getty

If you look up a dictionary of quotations you will find few reasons for a sensible man to desire to become wealthy.

—Robert Lynd

Superfluous wealth can buy superfluities only.

—Henry David Thoreau

Weather

Don't knock the weather; nine-tenths of the people couldn't start a conversation if it didn't change once in a while.

—Kin Hubbard

Sunshine is delicious, rain is refreshing, wind braces up, snow is exhilarating; there is no such thing as bad weather, only different kinds of good weather.

—John Ruskin

If you don't like the weather in New England, just wait a few minutes.

—Mark Twain

It was so cold the other day, I almost got married.

—Shelley Winters

Wickedness

See also: Evil

It is a statistical fact that the wicked work harder to reach hell than the righteous do to enter heaven.

—Josh Billings

I prefer the wicked rather than the foolish. The wicked sometimes rest.

—Alexandre Dumas pére

Some wicked people would be less dangerous had they no redeeming qualities.

—François, Duc de La Rochefoucauld

It is a fact that cannot be denied: the wickedness of others becomes our own wickedness because it kindles something evil in our own hearts.

—Carl Jung

Wickedness is a myth invented by good people to account for the curious attractiveness of others.

—Oscar Wilde

Wife

See also: Husband; Father; Marriage; Sex; Woman and Women

Many a man owes his success to his first wife and his second wife to his success.

—Jim Backus

A man's mother is his misfortune, but his wife is his fault.

—*Walter Bagehot*

Everybody all over the world takes a wife's estimate into account in forming an opinion of a man.

—*Honoré de Balzac*

He that displays too often his wife and his wallet is in danger of having both of them borrowed.

—*Benjamin Franklin*

The comfortable estate of widowhood is the only hope that keeps up a wife's spirits.

—*John Gay*

The best way of revenging yourself on a man who has stolen your wife is to leave her to him.

—*Sacha Guitry*

I am too much interested in other men's wives to think of getting one of my own.

—*George Moore*

Never feel remorse for what you have thought about your wife. She has thought much worse things about you.

—*Jean Rostand*

An ideal wife is any woman who has an ideal husband.

—*Booth Tarkington*

Will

See also: Ambition; Technology

The education of the will is the object of our existence.

—Ralph Waldo Emerson

To deny the freedom of the will is to make morality impossible.

—James A. Froude

He who is firm in will molds the world to himself.

—Goethe

People do not lack strength; they lack will.

—Victor Hugo

Wisdom

See also: Education; Judgment; Knowledge

All human wisdom is summed up in two words—wait and hope.

—Alexandre Dumas pére

History teaches us that men and nations behave wisely once they have exhausted all other alternatives.

—Abba Eban

It is the province of knowledge to speak, and it is the privilege of wisdom to listen.

—Oliver Wendell Holmes

Wisdom is early to despair.

—Gerard Manley Hopkins

The only medicine for suffering, crime, and all the other woes of mankind, is wisdom.

—Thomas Huxley

Some folks are wise, and some are otherwise.

—Tobias Smollett

He who is only wise lives a sad life.

—Voltaire

Wit

Wit ought to be a glorious treat, like caviar; never spread it about like marmalade.

—Noel Coward

Wit is a sword; it is meant to make people feel the point as well as see it.

—G. K. Chesterton

You can pretend to be serious; you can't pretend to be witty.

—Sacha Guitry

Wit is the salt of conversation, not the food.

—William Hazlitt

Wit lies in recognizing the resemblance among things which differ and the difference between things which are alike.

—Madame de Staël

Woman and Women

See also: Man and Men; Mother; Father; Marriage; Wife

Woman would be more charming if one could fall into her arms without falling into her hands.

—*Ambrose Bierce*

The way to fight a woman is with your hat. Grab it and run.

—*John Barrymore*

When she stopped conforming to the conventional picture of femininity, she finally began to enjoy being a woman.

—*Betty Friedan*

A woman may develop wrinkles and cellulite, lose her waistline, her bustline, her ability to bear a child, even her sense of humor, but none of that implies a loss of her sexuality, her femininity. . . .

—*Barbara Gordon*

Woman is at once apple and serpent.

—*Heinrich Heine*

Women who insist upon having the same options as men would do well to consider the option of being the strong, silent type.

—*Fran Lebowitz*

You don't know a woman until you have had a letter from her.

—*Ada Leverson*

The allurement that women hold out to men is precisely the allurement that Cape Hatteras holds out to sailors; they are enormously dangerous and hence enormously fascinating.

—H. L. Mencken

That woman speaks eighteen languages, and she can't say "No" in any of them.

—Dorothy Parker

Woman: the peg on which the wit hangs his jest, the preacher his text, the cynic his grouch and the sinner his justification.

—Helen Rowland

I hate women because they always know where things are.

—James Thurber

Whatever women do they must do it twice as well as men. Luckily, this is not difficult.

—Charlotte Whitton

A woman must have money and a room of her own.

—Virginia Woolf

Wonder

See also: Curiosity; Vision

It was through the feeling of wonder that men now and at first began to philosophize.

—Aristotle

Wonder is a basis of worship.

—Thomas Carlyle

He who can no longer pause to wonder and stand rapt in awe, is as good as dead; his eyes are closed.

—Albert Einstein

Men love to wonder and that is the seed of our science.

—Ralph Waldo Emerson

Words

See also: Arts: Writing; Books and Reading; Writers

Words are the physicians of a mind diseased.

—Aeschylus

A blow with a word strikes deeper than a blow with a sword.

—Robert Burton

Words without actions are the assassins of idealism.

—Herbert Hoover

Words are tools which automatically carve concepts out of experience.

—Julian S. Huxley

A thousand words will not leave so deep an impression as one deed.

—Henrik Ibsen

Words are the most powerful drug used by mankind.

—Rudyard Kipling

Unfortunately, sometimes people don't hear you until you scream.

—Stefanie Powers

Words are a lens to focus one's mind.

—Ayn Rand

One forgets words as one forgets names. One's vocabulary needs constant fertilization or it will die.

—Evelyn Waugh

Work

See also: Ambition; Labor

Nothing is really work unless you would rather be doing something else.

—J. M. Barrie

Anyone can do any amount of work, provided it isn't the work he's supposed to be doing at that moment.

—Robert Benchley

A man is a worker. If he is not that he is nothing.

—Joseph Conrad

The world is filled with willing people; some willing to work, the rest willing to let them.

—Robert Frost

The harder I work, the luckier I get.

—*Samuel Goldwyn*

Labor disgraces no man, but occasionally men disgrace labor.

—*Ulysses S. Grant*

I do not like work even when someone else does it.

—*Mark Twain*

World and Worldliness

The world is not growing worse and it is not growing better—it is just turning around as usual.

—*Finley Peter Dunne*

The world is a beautiful book, but of little use to him who cannot read.

—*Carlo Goldoni*

Worldliness is a spirit, a temperament, an attitude of the soul. . . . It is a gaze always horizontal and never vertical.

—*John Henry Jewett*

It's a man's world, and you men can have it.

—*Katherine Anne Porter*

The world is a comedy for those who think and a tragedy for those who feel.

—*Horace Walpole*

Anything that you love and do that keeps you from enjoying God's love and doing God's will is worldly and must be avoided.

—*Warren W. Wiersbe*

Writers

See also: Arts: Writing; Books and Reading

Writers aren't exactly people . . . they're a whole lot of people trying to be one person.

—*F. Scott Fitzgerald*

One man is as good as another until he has written a book.

—*Benjamin Jowett*

Only a mediocre writer is always at his best.

—*W. Somerset Maugham*

Writers don't need love. All they require is money.

—*John Osborne*

The dubious privilege of a freelance writer is he's given the freedom to starve anywhere.

—*S. J. Perelman*

Why did I write? Because I found life unsatisfactory.

—*Tennessee Williams*

Y

Youth

In youth we run into difficulties, in old age difficulties run into us.

—*Josh Billings*

When the waitress puts the dinner on the table, the old men look at the dinner. The young men look at the waitress.

—*Gelett Burgess*

The young always have the same problem—how to rebel and conform at the same time. They have now solved this by defying their parents and copying one another.

—*Quentin Crisp*

Almost everything that is great has been done by youth.

—*Benjamin Disraeli*

Youth is the best time to be rich, and the best time to be poor.

—*Euripides*

Youth is a wonderful thing. What a crime to waste it on children.

—*George Bernard Shaw*

No wise man every wished to be younger.

—*Jonathan Swift*

Z

Zeal

See also: Ambition; Enthusiasm

Never let your zeal outrun your charity. The former is but human, the latter is divine.

—*Hosea Ballou*

The greatest dangers to liberty lurk in insidious encroachment by men of zeal, well-meaning, but without understanding.

—*Louis D. Brandeis*

Zeal without humanity is like a ship without a rudder, liable to be stranded at any moment.

—*Owen Felltham*

To be furious in religion is to be irreligiously religious.

—*William Penn*

Zeal is very blind, or badly regulated, when it encroaches upon the rights of others.

—*Quesnel*